Robert Burns
His Personality, His Reputation and His Art

Robert Burns

His Personality, His Reputation and His Art

By Franklyn Bliss Snyder

KENNIKAT PRESS
Port Washington, N. Y./London

ROBERT BURNS

First published in 1936
Reissued in 1970 by Kennikat Press
Library of Congress Catalog Card No: 73-95332
ISBN 0-8046-1348-6

Manufactured by Taylor Publishing Company   Dallas, Texas

I

His Personality

IN one of his many letters to Mrs. Dunlop, Burns reminded his most insistent correspondent that "[this] is so exhausted a subject that any new idea on the business is not to be expected; 'tis well if we can place an old idea in a new light." May I reaffirm this statement as a pertinent headnote to what I am about to say concerning Burns. Ever since that July day in 1786 when the Kilmarnock edition—one of the most notable "first volumes" in the chronicle of English literature—came from the press of John Wilson, Burns's character and accomplishments have been the subjects of almost uninterrupted discussion. In addition to those whom one might call his professional editors and biographers, Burns has had a long and distinguished list of commentators and interpreters. Byron and Wordsworth, Goethe and Carlyle, Jeffrey and Scott, Arnold, Stevenson, Whitman, Lowell, Emerson, and Henley, are by no means all of the better known writers who have fallen under the charm of his personality and his verse, and have commented understandingly on his poetry and his life. More recently, scholars and bibliographers have found the voluminous Burns literature a rich field in which to exercise their talents, and have shown how much remains to be done towards clearing up old errors and laying the bases for sound generalizations. Scotsmen the world around have scrutinized zealously whatever has been published about him, and have been assiduous in their search for anything that might increase our knowledge of the poet and his world. And each successive year has brought its spate of less scholarly but highly significant comment: the birthday addresses, sermons, and poems; the letters to the Edinburgh *Scotsman* and the Glasgow *Herald*, which, taken together, give abundant evidence of the enduring nature of Burns's hold upon the affections of English-speaking people. The "old idea" has thus been so many times viewed "in a new light", that one wonders whether more than a pretext of novelty can to-day be imparted to any reinterpretation of Burns and his poetry.

None the less, I propose to make the attempt; to subject Burns to such concentrated rays of critical speculation as I am capable of focussing upon him, in the hope that I may say something about his personality, his reputation, and his art, which will not be merely a re-stating of facts better set forth by some of my many predecessors in this fascinating field of study.

Burns's funeral, a military pageant arranged by his friend John Syme, took place at Dumfries on

Monday, July 25, 1796. Within three weeks of that day there appeared in the Dumfries *Journal* a character sketch, signed "Candidior", of which one may still say what Henley and Henderson said forty years ago: it "remains the best thing written of him by contemporary critic". From this sketch, the work of a woman whom Burns had loved and affronted, and who had forgiven the insult while treasuring the memory of some years of intimate friendship, I cull one sentence: "Mr. Burns", she wrote, "had an irresistible power of attraction." "An irresistible power of attraction": in those five words Mrs. Walter Riddell stated once and for all one of the significant facts concerning Robert Burns. For the charm of which Mrs. Riddell and Burns's other friends were conscious, has persisted through the hundred and forty years that have elapsed since his death. We ourselves, though denied the privilege of meeting him face to face, still feel the attraction of his vivid personality, speaking to us through the pages of his prose and verse; and we know that our children's children will feel it after us.

Mrs. Riddell made little attempt to analyse or explain this "irresistible attraction". She was content, wisely perhaps, to state the fact, and to leave to future questioners the task of probing more deeply into the mystery of Burns's personality. And the task is not an easy one, for mystery that personality was and still is. How came this son of William Burnes to grow to such stature that the world looks at him in amaze, when all his brothers and sisters, yes, and all his children as well, are known only because of their relationship to him? What pattern did the gods use when they shaped his soul? What is the secret that made Burns the best loved of all the greater English poets?

Carlyle, with his uncanny skill at human portraiture, singled out sincerity as Burns's fundamental characteristic; Henley, coiner of memorable phrases, called him "a faun of genius". Both statements are partial truths, but neither goes to the heart of the problem. For Burns's personality was so many-sided, and some aspects of it seem so contradictory, that any attempt to tag him with a single phrase is bound to result in failure. In December of 1813 Byron read a sheaf of what he called Burns's "unpublished and never-to-be-published" letters, probably addressed to a fellow-member of the Crochallan Fencibles, and wrote thus in his *Journal* of the impression they made on him: "What an antithetical mind!—tenderness, roughness—delicacy, coarseness—sentiment, sensuality—soaring and grovelling, dirt and deity—all mixed up in that one compound of inspired clay." An "antithetical mind". Anyone who cares to, can go through Burns's letters and find in them good evidence that he was joyous and melancholy, courageous and panic-stricken, independent and obsequious, proud and humble, tenderly compassionate and meanly vituperative; that he glorified honest poverty but dreaded it almost beyond any other human misfortune, and that throughout his entire mature life he displayed qualities whose very nature would seem to preclude the existence of other qualities as easily discernible in the tissue of his soul.

In part, of course, these paradoxes are explained by the fact of Burns's health. One remembers that when the devil was sick, the devil a monk would be. Now Burns, as recent medical research has made clear, suffered from that lingering form of heart disease called endocarditis; in addition, he was a life-long victim of what he named "a deep, incurable taint of hypochondria". When he was well, he was the Burns whom Edinburgh lionized, whom Dumfries claimed as one of her most honoured burgesses, and who talked and laughed and sang his way into the affections of all who really knew him. But when he was ill, and the "blue-devils" arose to plague him, he became the Burns who cried to Bob Ainslie in despair, "Canst thou not minister to a mind diseased"; who wrote to Peggy Chalmers, "God have mercy on me! a poor, damned, duped, incautious fool! The sport, the miserable victim, of rebellious pride, hypochondriac imagination, agonizing sensibility, and bedlam passion"; and who later told the same sympathetic correspondent that as he thought over the events of the past two years he could "sit down and cry like a child!" Well, he was the Burns of *Contented wi' Little an' Cantie wi' Mair;* ill, the Burns of the *Prayer under the Pressure of Violent Anguish;* well, he could forget an affront and forgive the offender; ill, he could write ungenerous epigrams on friends who had done him no real wrong, and circulate copies with spiteful glee. Well, he could remind Mrs. Dunlop of "that peculiar good luck that for some years past has attended all my efforts"; ill, he could as sincerely tell Peter Stuart that "A damned star has almost all my life usurped my zenith, and squinted out the cursed rays of its malign influences. In the strong language of the old Hebrew Seer—'And behold, whatsoever he purposeth, it shall not come to pass; and whatsoever he doeth, it shall not prosper'."

In trying to reconcile such apparent inconsistencies in Burns's character, one should never forget that the last twelve or fifteen years of his life were spent in a losing struggle with the malady that was to bring him to his early grave, and that three times serious bodily accidents rendered him a virtually helpless cripple. During the many periods of illness or physical incapacitation Burns's spirits sank to pathetically low ebbs, and he wrote and said and did things that seem utterly out of keeping with the character manifested during his happy intervals of freedom from disease and pain.

But even if Burns had lived his allotted span of years in unbroken physical and mental health, it is doubtful whether he could have kept himself free from moody periods of depression. For Burns's most harassing problem was not that of health, important as this certainly was. It was the problem of how to accommodate the spirit of a great and original genius in the narrowly circumscribed world of a small tenant farmer and district exciseman. This problem Burns never wholly solved; in the language of the sociologist, the genius remained somewhat "maladjusted". The consciousness of this fact brought inevitable hours of regret—regret that was sometimes wistful, and sometimes passionately rebellious. Burns was well aware of his poetic abilities; aware that it was in his power to do what only genius can accomplish. His ambition—his poetic, artistic ambition—was unbounded. But Fate compelled him to expend most of his energy in toiling for his daily bread, and thus estopped him, as he thought, from giving full expression to the urge for artistic creation. Because he was aware of this repression, there developed in him a lurking consciousness of failure —a consciousness which, however unjustified it may seem in the light of what Burns actually accomplished, goes far towards explaining his recurring periods of gloom. And I do not believe it is stretching the point too much to associate part at least of the "occasional hard drinking" which Burns told Mrs. Dunlop was "the devil to [him]" with a quite understandable desire to find respite from the accusations of his artistic conscience.

Parenthetically, one wonders what would have been the result if Fate had gratified Burns with the "life of literary leisure with a decent competence" which he said was "the summit of [his] wishes". Suppose that, like Shelley or the young Milton, he had been free from the iron necessity of daily toil, or that like Wordsworth he had been enabled to withdraw at the age of twenty-nine from the disturbing world of men and affairs, and to round out four score years in quiet seclusion; would the poetic result have been more distinguished than that which we know? Would Burns's *Complete Works* have contained a dramatic poem more notable than *The Jolly Beggars*, or lyrics more tender, more nearly perfect, than *John Anderson* and *Bonie Doon*, or narratives more brilliant than *Tam*? Who can answer such questions! Personally I believe it was the very necessity of living at close grips with labour and suffering, two of the fundamental and inescapable facts of human experience, that enabled Burns to write so that whoever has known either of these two experiences can find in him sympathy and consolation and courage and good cheer. Personally I believe that if Burns's genius had not been forced to accommodate itself to the hard life of tenant farmer and exciseman, his poetry might have lacked the bone and fibre that give it its sinewy strength. The fact that he was compelled to fight against heavy odds prevented him from deteriorating into a Scottish Shenstone or a second Allan Ramsay, of no lasting significance either human or artistic. All this, however, is somewhat beside the point; for I do not propose to engage in speculation as to what might have happened—if!

To return, then, to the problem under discussion—the paradoxical, antithetical, mysterious, and altogether fascinating personality of Robert Burns; the stuff of which had been moulded by long centuries of border-raiding, of warfare waged for national independence, of conflict between Pope and Presbyter, and of the unending struggle to wrest a living from the stubborn soil of poorly tilled Scottish lowlands.

A hundred years ago there were readers of Burns who believed this problem had been forever solved. In March of 1834, Burns's grave in St. Michael's kirkyard was opened, and the body of Jean Armour was laid to rest beside that of her husband. Certain zealous believers in what was then called the science of phrenology seized the opportunity to make—surreptitiously, it would seem—a cast of Burns's skull. When the deed had been done and the measurements completed, the results were announced to the world. "Philoprogenitiveness, adhesiveness, combativeness, love of approbation, and benevolence"—these were the qualities, among some twenty-odd, which the investigators decided had been most fully developed in Burns; least marked of his personal traits had been "number, order, and hope".

The problem is not quite so easily solved as these "scientists" would have had us believe. Indeed, I doubt whether much would be gained by following the lead of our phrenological predecessors and listing the personal qualities that appear reflected in Burns's prose and verse, as they catalogued the results of their cranial measurements. It would not be hard to do, and one could cite chapter and verse in support of each entry. Pride, passion, sentimentalism, generosity, recklessness, courage, sympathy—such would be some of the entries. But these qualities of Burns's personality have been pointed out many a time; little profit can come from re-telling an old tale. Moreover, no matter how extensive one might make such a list, something would always be missing—the mysterious x in the equation; the unknown quantity that made Burns, Burns. It will be less certainly productive of futility to avoid any attempt at inclusiveness in our analysis, and to consider one prominent trait in Burns's personality that seems never to have been adequately recognized, his intellectual power. By limiting ourselves to a consideration of this single characteristic, we shall at least avoid the pitfall of discursiveness; and we may perhaps find one good reason for the enduring significance of Burns's poetry.

In thus ascribing to Burns notable intellectual power, I mean much more than that he impresses me as a man endowed by Nature with great mental ability. He does indeed make this impression; in fact, I wonder sometimes whether he ever met his equal in this respect. If he did, I cannot name the man. Not Hugh Blair, nor Henry Erskine, nor Adam Ferguson, nor even Dugald Stewart; hardly Walter Scott, whom Burns saw, a lad in his teens, at Ferguson's home. But Burns was not content merely to possess an unusual mental equipment; he used it. The astonishing range of his vocabulary would alone be good proof of his mental activity. No person with a sluggish mind could have used words as Burns used them. An exposition of his interest in music, which most critics have overlooked, would throw interesting light upon this phase of his personality, but can hardly be undertaken without recourse to such minute technicalities as would be inappropriate here. His knowledge of English literature, his thorough acquaintance with the mysteries of Scottish theological dogma and ecclesiastical history, his veritable mastery of the fascinating but bewildering field of Scottish song—any one of these accomplishments might be cited to the same end, and a large amount of evidence could be assembled on each point. But most of these facts have been often commented on. Hence I content myself with pointing out three slightly less obvious but equally significant indications of Burns's intellectual range and power. First, he was alert and inquisitive about history and politics, matters that lay far beyond the horizon of the average Scottish farmer in 1785. Second, he had an unusual talent for reducing things to their lowest terms, for coming swiftly to the heart of a matter, and for reasoning from the known to the unknown—or, if you will, for seeing the ultimate as well as the immediate significance of facts. Finally, in his continuous and life-long scrutiny of himself, he displayed an incisive accuracy of observation so combined with an impersonal detachment, or objectivity, as to render his feats of self-analysis perhaps the most significant evidence of his mental ability.

Consider the first of these three matters. To open any volume of Burns's letters, is to see him as a student of history and politics. A playful sentence from the vivacious letter to John Arnot, written nine months before the publication of the Kilmarnock volume, shows how easily the young poet could draw analogies from history—Biblical, classical, mediaeval European, and American—and cap them with an apt quotation from *Hamlet:*

> I was utterly routed, my baggage lost, my military chest in the hands of the enemy. . . . In short, Pharaoh at the Red Sea, Darius at Arbela, Pompey at Pharsalia, Edward at Bannockburn, Burgoyne at Saratoga—no Prince, Potentate, or Commander of ancient or modern unfortunate memory, ever got a more shameful or total defeat—
>
> O horrible! O horrible! Most horrible!

Three years later, in November of 1788, and in far more serious vein, Burns wrote to the Edinburgh *Evening Courant,* protesting against the "harsh and abusive manner" in which the House of Stuart had been characterized by the clergyman conducting the exercises held on November 5 to commemorate the "great and glorious revolution". Two paragraphs from the published letter illustrate so admirably both Burns's political interests and his ability to write lucid and vigorous prose, that I quote them both:

> "The bloody and tyrannical house of Stuart" may be said with propriety and justice, when compared with the present Royal Family, and the liberal sentiments of our days. But is there no allowance to be made for

the manners of the times? Were the royal contemporaries of the Stuarts more mildly attentive to the rights of man? Might not the epithets of "bloody and tyrannical" be with at least equal justice applied to the house of Tudor, or York, or any other of their predecessors?

Man, Mr. Printer, is a strange, weak, inconsistent being. . . . Who would believe, Sir, that in this our Augustan age of liberality and refinement, while we seem so justly sensible and jealous of our rights and liberties, and animated with such indignation against the very memory of those who would have subverted them, who would suppose that a certain people, under our national protection, should complain not against a Monarch and a few favourite advisers, but against our whole legislative body,—and almost in the very same terms as our forefathers did against the House of Stuart! I will not, I cannot, enter into the merits of the cause; but I dare say the American Congress, in 1776, will be allowed to have been as able and as enlightened, and, a whole Empire will say, as honest, as the English Convention in 1688; and that the fourth of July will be as sacred to their posterity as the fifth of November is to us.

These paragraphs were not the sentimental effusions of a pseudo-Jacobite; only a man who knew a good deal and thought incisively could have written them. They would have done credit to Burke or Franklin.

Or listen to Burns's letter to Alexander Cunningham, written in February of the nervous year 1793:

> What are you doing, what hurry have you got on your hands, my dear Cunningham, that I have not heard from you? Are you deeply engaged in the mazes of Law, the mysteries of Love, or in the profound wisdom of modern Politics? Curse on the word which ended the period!
> Quere. What is Politics?
> Answer. Politics is a science wherewith, by means of nefarious cunning and hypocritical pretense, we govern civil Polities for the emolument of ourselves and our adherents.
> Quere. What is a Minister?
> Answer. A Minister is an unprincipled fellow, who by the influence of hereditary or acquired wealth, by superiour abilities, or by a lucky conjuncture of circumstances, obtains a principal place in the administration of the affairs of government.
> Quere. What is a Patriot?
> Answer. An individual exactly of the same description as a Minister, only out of place.

Once again the mingling of irony and sarcasm and truth suggests Franklin.

Towards the close of 1794 a casual comment on the execution of Louis XVI and Marie Antoinette cost Burns the friendship of Mrs. Dunlop, two of whose sons-in-law were French royalist refugees, but gives us further evidence of both his power of phrase and his attention to historical and political developments:

> I cannot approve of [Dr. Moore's] whining over the deserved fate of a certain pair of Personages. . . .

> What is there in the delivering over a perjured Blockhead and an unprincipled Prostitute to the hands of the hangman, that it should arrest for a moment attention in an eventful hour when, as my friend Roscoe in Liverpool so gloriously expresses it,
> The welfare of millions is hung in the scale,
> And the balance yet trembles with fate.

Then, turning swiftly to British affairs, and recalling the repressive measures promulgated during the months of panic, he adds: "Thank God these London trials have given us a little more breath, and I imagine that the time is not far distant when a man may freely blame Willy Pitt, without being called an enemy to his Country."

A single allusion to Adam Smith, who had subscribed for four copies of Burns's first Edinburgh edition, and had even suggested finding a position for the poet in the Salt Office, is interesting in this connection, though the letter was written before the storming of the Bastille. Burns is addressing his friend and patron on the Excise Board, Robert Graham of Fintry:

> By the by, the Excise-instructions were not in the bundle.—But 'tis no matter; Marshall in his *Yorkshire*, and particularly that extraordinary man Smith, in his *Wealth of Nations*, find my leisure employment enough. I could not have given any mere *man* credit for half the intelligence Mr. Smith discovers in his book. I would covet much to have his ideas respecting the present state of some quarters of the world that are or have

been the scenes of considerable revolution since his book was written.

Passages such as these—and their number could be generously increased—one rarely finds outside the writings of professed students of history and politics. That Burns, burdened as he was with the cares of the day, found time and energy to consider such matters, and to comment on them with astuteness, is good evidence of the quality of his intellect—insatiable in its curiosity, and swiftly accurate in its workings.

The poems, too, show the same phase of Burns's intellectual interests. One may overlook such political satire as appears in *The Twa Dogs;* it is vague and general, hardly above the level of a Hyde Park orator with a gift of phrase. In *The Author's Earnest Cry and Prayer* Burns is more specific, and shows that he is keenly observant of the activities of the Scottish representatives in the House of Commons. Even so, however, the poem displays no sure mark of intellectual distinction. *A Fragment: "When Guilford Good"* is of a different stamp. Here are nine stanzas that would tax the learning of any annotator; stanzas that give a swift *résumé* of the entire American war, that summarize cabinet changes in England over a number of years, and comment shrewdly on the personal attributes of a score of military and political leaders. No one could have written the poem who was not acutely attentive to political history, and at the same time blessed with a consummate mastery of ballad technique.

Let me cite one more poem from the many that witness Burns's concern over politics, the epistle *To a Gentleman who had Lent a Newspaper*. It is neither long nor well-known; with certain unimportant omissions it runs thus:

> Kind Sir, I've read your paper through,
> And faith, to me 'twas really new!
> How guessed ye, Sir, what maist I wanted?
> This monie a day I've grained and gaunted,
> To ken what French mischief was brewin;
> Or what the drumlie Dutch were doin;
> That vile doup-skelper, Emperor Joseph,
> If Venus yet had got his nose off;
> Or how the collieshangie works
> Atween the Russians and the Turks;
> Or if the Swede, afore he halt,
> Would play anither Charles the Twalt;
> If Denmark, any body spak o't,
> Or Poland, wha had now the tack o't;
> How cut-throat Prussian blades were hingin;
> How libbet Italy was singin;
> If Spaniard, Portuguese, or Swiss
> Were sayin or takin aught amiss;
> Or how our merry lads at hame
> In Britain's court kept up the game:
> How royal George—the Lord leuk o'er him!—
> Was managing St. Stephen's quorum;
> If sleekit Chatham Will was livin,
> Or glaikit Charlie got his nieve in;

> How Daddie Burke the plea was cookin;
> If Warren Hastings' neck was yeukin;
> The news o' princes, dukes, and earls,
> Pimps, sharpers, bawds, and opera-girls;
>
> * * * * *
>
> A' this and mair I never heard of,
> And, but for you, I might despair'd of.
> So, gratefu', back your news I send you,
> And pray a' guid things may attend you.

Here, within the compass of sixteen octosyllabic couplets, Burns glances at France, Holland, Austria, Russia, Turkey, Sweden, Denmark, Poland, Prussia, Italy, Spain, Portugal, and Switzerland, and asks pertinent questions concerning developments in England. Furthermore, he does it all with an ease that speaks eloquently for his astonishing fluency in verse, and his familiarity with the matters under discussion.

Excerpts like these show Burns's interest in politics and history, and the quality of his thinking when he was considering such matters. But only when one follows him over the course of many years can one realize how large a part they played in his intellectual life. He was attentive to purely local problems, such as the choice of a representative for the Dumfries boroughs; he followed developments at Westminster almost as keenly as if he himself had been a member of Parliament; and always he was conscious that beyond the confines of Britain, as well as within them, forces were at work which promised "greater happiness to all mankind". It was not his fortune to brood over the 1792 September massacres in a "high and lonely" room of a Parisian hotel, or to number among his friends such an eloquent apologist for the Revolution as Michel Beaupuis. But even without the stimulus of that close physical association which Wordsworth enjoyed, Burns was thoroughly conversant with affairs in France, and became, as he put it, "her enthusiastic votary in the beginning of the business". To be sure, this Scottish farmer and exciseman never permitted his interest in international affairs to distract him from the task in hand. He cared for his family and drained his tillage and cast up his accounts with scrupulous attention to the demands of the hour. Ellisland's hundred and seventy acres, the ten parishes over which he rode as a gauger, the town of Dumfries—these formed the physical scene of Burns's last eight years. But when the day's work was done, the horizon of his life expanded to include all Europe and America, and he lived and thought as an alert and keen-minded citizen of the world.

I turn next to Burns's ability to reduce complicated matters to simple terms, and to use past and present as bases for accurate forecasts of the future. There are few better tests of any man's mental power than these: to require him to select the two or three essentials from a mass of heterogeneously related facts, and to ask him to reason accurately from the known to the unknown. The first is the task of the lumberman who drives his pike-pole into the "key-log" and breaks the jam; the second is the task which all of us perform—or fail to perform—in foretelling the events of tomorrow. In both, Burns showed himself not unskilled.

Certain of the passages I have cited in connection with Burns's attention to politics would serve equally well as evidence of his ability to seize upon the essential features of a complex problem. But it will be interesting, in this connection, to turn to a somewhat different field, and look at two of his many comments on "Auld Licht" Calvinism. It is not difficult for the critic of to-day to emulate Browning's duke, and with deft precision show the Calvinist that

> Just this
> Or that in you disgusts me; here you miss,
> Or there exceed the mark.

So many persons, during the last century, have found satisfaction in exposing what they thought to be the faults of Calvinistic theology, that to-day any tyro in disputation can turn the trick. But in 1785, in Scotland, the task was more difficult. The Kirk was still virtually all-powerful; her legal position seemed impregnable, the validity of her dogmas unquestionable. The very magnificence of her history, her superb record of endurance in the face of persecution, were enough to overawe most objectors. Then too, as Dr. Holmes pointed out in *The One-Hoss-Shay*, there were no obviously weak spots in her creedal armour. But Burns was not to be deterred by an imposing organization or an invincible logic. The giant might be a real giant to other people; to him it was only a windmill, to be attacked unhesitatingly.

For example, in the summer of 1789 Dr. William M'Gill, one of the two ministers at Ayr, was in difficulty because of the liberal sentiments expressed in his *Practical Essay on the Death of Jesus Christ*. Burns commented on the affair thus, in a letter to Graham of Fintry:

> God help him, poor man! Though he is one of the worthiest as well as one of the ablest of the whole priesthood of the Kirk of Scotland,—yet for the blasphemous heresies of squaring Religion by the rules of Common Sense, and attempting to give a decent character to Almighty God, and a rational account of his proceedings with the Sons of Men, the poor Doctor and his numerous family are in imminent danger of being thrown out to the mercy of the winter wind.

There, in one sentence, are the fundamental defects of eighteenth-century Calvinism. It failed to give "a decent character to Almighty God" or "a rational account of his proceedings with the Sons of Men".

Or take *Holy Willie's Prayer.* Here Burns is not merely holding up to scorn a specific individual; he is satirizing the harsh and unlovely dogmas of the entire system that William Fisher represented. Juvenal himself might well have envied Burns the restrained, mordant, and superbly analytic first five stanzas:

> O Thou that in the Heavens does dwell,
> Wha, as it pleases best Thysel,
> Sends ane to Heaven an' ten to Hell
>   A' for Thy glory,
> And no for onie guid or ill
>   They've done before Thee!
>
> I bless and praise Thy matchless might,
> When thousands Thou has left in night,
> That I am here before Thy sight,
>   For gifts an' grace
> A burning and a shining light
>   To a' this place.
>
> What was I, or my generation,
> That I should get sic exaltation?
> I, wha deserv'd most just damnation
>   For broken laws
> Sax thousand years ere my creation,
>   Thro' Adam's cause!
>
> When from my mither's womb I fell
> Thou might hae plung'd me deep in hell
> To gnash my gooms, and weep, and wail
>   In burning lakes,
> Where damned devils roar and yell,
>   Chain'd to their stakes.

> Yet I am here, a chosen sample,
> To show Thy grace is great and ample:
> I'm here, a pillar o' Thy temple,
> > Strong as a rock,
> A guide, a buckler, and example
> > To a' Thy flock!

I doubt whether anyone has ever shown the ultimate implications of the doctrines of original sin, universal damnation, and election, more effectively than Burns exposed them in those thirty short lines of verse. And only a man of genuine intellectual power could have written those lines. It was in admiration of Burns's skill in this sort of criticism that Emerson once wrote: "Not Latimer, nor Luther, struck more telling blows against false theology than did this brave singer."

One further illustration of Burns's ability to reduce things to their lowest terms will not be superfluous. In the winter of 1788 Burns and Mrs. Agnes M'Lehose—"Clarinda"—were involved in their tempestuous love affair, and despite all Clarinda's attempts at concealment, people had begun to talk. In particular, Dr. John Kemp, minister of the Canongate Church, and Lord Justice Craig, Clarinda's kinsman, seem to have been outspoken in remonstrance. The church held it a sin for a married woman to comport herself as Clarinda was doing; the law, represented by Lord Craig, was equally sure that her conduct was on the point of becoming criminal. But neither lawyer nor preacher saw to the heart of the matter. That was reserved for the poet himself, who made it quite clear to Clarinda why such entanglements had best be avoided:

> Had we never lov'd sae kindly,
> Had we never lov'd sae blindly,
> Never met, or never parted,
> We had ne'er been broken hearted.

There is no word of sin or crime here, but only the reminder that out of love like theirs come broken hearts, and little else. Could anyone have told the truth more simply and more accurately?

If anything could have weakened Burns's intellectual fibre and upset his mental balance, the first winter in Edinburgh might well have done it. To rise suddenly from obscurity to fame, to find the world of wealth and society and culture quite literally at his feet, might have "spoiled" Burns, as some of his acquaintances predicted it would. But not once during that triumphant and trying experience did he lose his poise. Even while the applause was at its height he was carefully laying plans for the future, and looking ahead not to the career of a professional man of letters, but to the humble occupation of farmer or gauger. He was not deluded into thinking that a pendulum could swing always in one direction, and never forgot that action and reaction are equal—and opposite.

From the many pertinent passages in Burns's letters that show him thinking clear-headedly about the future, reasoning from the known to the unknown, I select two that are characteristic of the entire group. The first is from a letter to Mrs. Dunlop:

> You are afraid I shall grow intoxicated with my prosperity as a Poet: alas! Madam, I know myself and the world too well. . . . I am willing to believe that my abilities deserve some notice; but . . . to be dragged forth to the full glare of learned and polite observation, with all my imperfections of awkward rusticity . . . on my head—I assure you, Madam, I do not dissemble when I tell you I tremble for the consequences. The novelty of a poet in my obscure situation . . . has raised a partial tide of public notice which has borne me to a height where I am . . . certain my abilities are inadequate to support me; and too surely do I see that time when the same tide will leave me, and recede, perhaps as far below the level of truth.

A little later he wrote to William Dunbar: "The time is approaching when I shall return to my shades; and I am afraid my numerous Edinburgh friendships are of so tender a construction that they will not bear carriage with me." The tide of popularity did recede; and of all the people who had sought his friendship during the months in Edinburgh, only three, Cleghorn, Cunningham, and Peter Hill, maintained it unbroken to the end of Burns's life.

Or consider this whole matter of Burns's Edinburgh experiences. When he abandoned his proposed trip to Jamaica and went up to the capital to win fame, his chances of success were approximately what they would have been had he undertaken single-handed to scale Castle Rock and batter his way through barred gateway and portcullis. But he planned his campaign shrewdly, carried it through triumphantly, and gave final proof of his good sense by striking his tents and returning to the country before Edinburgh's enthusiasm had begun to wane. All this, I suggest, indicates a level head and clear thinking on the part of an inexperienced young man who had every reason to be unbalanced by his success.

Still another indication of Burns's intellectual power appears in his ability to examine himself with commendable objectivity, and to state his findings with frankness and accuracy. He was all his life interested in men and women, but was especially concerned with the one person whom he knew best, and who chanced, between 1785 and 1796, to be perhaps the most interesting human being in the British Isles. Relatively early in life he had begun keeping a Commonplace Book because he thought "it might be some entertainment to a curious observer of human nature to see how a Ploughman thinks and feels". To make the record of his thoughts and feelings reasonably accurate, he spent many an hour in self-examination. The introspective habit thus developed—or, rather, thus made manifest—carried over to the end of his life, and to the day of his death one finds Burns thinking much about himself. His health, his daily occupations, his ideals of conduct, his practice (often distinctly at variance with his ideals), his religious opinions, his standards of taste, his hopes, his disappointments—everything that entered into his life, passed within range of his critical gaze. As a result, he could write to his friend Robert Aiken that "I know pretty exactly what ground I occupy both as a Man and a Poet".

But he was not satisfied with merely knowing himself; he must set down in words the results of his scrutiny. For Burns was one of those people—should we not call them fortunate?—who are born to hold a pen, and who can never be content till they have seen their own experiences take shape on the written page. Consequently his prose and verse, significant as they are for many other reasons, are of continuing interest because they contain his own colourful portrait of himself—sincere, unblushing, inclusive, and so accurate in its delineations that Burns was and always will remain his own best interpreter.

There is so much evidence of Burns's skill in self-analysis that one hardly knows where to turn first for illustrations. One thinks of the autobiographical letter to Dr. Moore, rich in facts and accurate in interpretation—a unique document in Burns's prose, the sort of record that every poet should be required to leave behind for the guidance of future biographers. But more interesting in some ways are the casual remarks, the "asides", so to speak, that appear on page after page of his correspondence. For example: "I am the sport of whim, caprice, and passion"; or, "I know myself, and how far I can depend on [my] passions, well. It has been my particular study"; or, "There was ever but one side on which I was habitually blameable, and there I have secured myself in the way pointed out by Nature"; or, "I like to hear myself speak"; or, "I am not very amenable to counsel". At greater length, but with the same engaging frankness, he wrote to Peter Hill:

> God knows I am no saint, and I have a whole host of Follies and Sins to answer for; but if I could, and I believe I do it as far as I can, I would wipe away all tears from all eyes. Even the knaves who have injured me, I would oblige them; tho' to tell the truth, it would be more out of vengeance, to show them that I was independent of, and above them, than out of the overflowings of my benevolence.

To Robert Aiken he once wrote: "I am sometimes pleased with myself in my grateful sensations; but I believe, on the whole, I have very little merit in it, as my gratitude is not a virtue, the consequence of reflection; but sheerly the instinctive emotion of my heart." And again: "You see, Sir, that if to *know* one's errors were a probability of *mending* them, I stand a fair chance: but, according to the reverend Westminster divines, though conviction must precede conversion, it is very far from always implying it." Finally, take this delightful confession, made in the autumn of 1793 to Robert Cleghorn: "There is, there must be, some truth in original sin.—My violent propensity to bawdy convinces me of it."

These are random but typical examples of the results of Burns's self-examination. Any reader of the prose can add to the list as he sees fit. And the chief significance of these utterances is not that Burns made such comments on himself, but that, tested in the light of all that we know of him, they seem astonishingly accurate.

The poems like the letters show that Burns needed no admonition to look in his heart and write. Sometimes, as in the unpoetic but sincere *Bard's Epitaph*, he characterized himself directly:

> A man whose judgment clear
> Can others teach the course to steer,
> Yet runs, himself, life's mad career
>   Wild as the wave.

Sometimes, as in *A Poet's Welcome to his Lovebegotten Daughter*, one of the most wistfully appealing of all Burns's personal lyrics, he combines this sort of self-portraiture with an indirect presentation of what one might call his attitude towards many things. One stanza in particular is interesting, for it shows Burns enjoying the "publicity" he was receiving:

> What tho' they ca' me fornicator,
>   An' tease my name in kintra clatter?
> The mair they talk, I'm kend the better;
>   E'en let them clash!
> An auld wife's tongue's a feckless matter
>   To gie ane fash.

Sometimes, as in the *Address to the Unco Guid*, he says little about himself except by implication; the entire poem, however, is Burns's apology for his own life, and was written only after long introspection. The last three stanzas are the most significant in this connection:

> Think, when your castigated pulse
>   Gies now and then a wallop,
> What ragings must his veins convulse
>   That still eternal gallop!
> Wi' wind and tide fair i' your tail,
>   Right on ye scud your seaway;
> But in the teeth o' baith to sail,
>   Ye mak an unco' leeway.
>
> Then gently scan your brother man,
>   Still gentler sister woman;
> Tho' they may gang a kennin wrang,
>   To step aside is human:

> One point must still be greatly dark,
>   The moving *why* they do it;
> And just as lamely can ye mark
>   How far perhaps they rue it.
>
> Who made the heart, tis He alone
>   Decidedly can try us;
> He knows each chord its various tone,
>   Each spring its various bias:
> Then at the balance let's be mute,
>   We never can adjust it;
> What's done we partly may compute,
>   But know not what's resisted.

The *Epistle to a Young Friend*, as the author realized, is part "sang" and part "sermon"; the sermon is in effect an exposition of Burns's philosophy of life, and is based on an examination of his own conduct. The concluding song in *The Jolly Beggars* should not be interpreted as Burns speaking in his own person; none the less it is the ultimate expression of the rebellious side of Burns's personality:

> A fig for those by law protected,
>   Liberty's a glorious feast;
> Courts for cowards were erected,
>   Churches built to please the priest.

But one need not particularize further. Page after page of the poems, and not a few of the songs, witness the care with which Burns scrutinized himself, and the accuracy with which he delineated various aspects of his character, and thus gave further evidence of his intellectual power.

Burns's personality had, of course, many more facets than those I have touched upon even incidentally. I have not mentioned his devotion to his kindred, his love of fun, his sense of humour, his business acumen, his innate friendliness. The facts I have tried to set forth have not been in any sense startling. They illustrate a distinctly less spectacular aspect of the poet's character than others that might as easily have been pointed out, and for that very reason have been little talked about during the century and a half in which the old idea has been viewed in a new light. But not till one realizes what I have tried to suggest, the power and range of Burns's intellect, and the accuracy of his thinking, will one come even near to understanding the man or his enduring appeal.

For there are only two accomplishments that the world marks as of supreme merit. "Find out something that is true", we might well say to our young friends on university campuses, "or make something that is beautiful, if you wish your names to be remembered." Many people have pointed out Burns's skill in shaping the twenty-six letters of the alphabet into patterns of haunting beauty. I suggest that by virtue of his intellectual power wedded to this gift of song he became one of the few whose fortune it is to unite Truth and Beauty, and thus to bestow on humanity the most satisfying of all boons. I suggest that in the exercise of his intellectual talents he displayed an intuitive instinct for veracity that explains much of the continuing appeal of his poetry, and that sets him off sharply from all other modern Scottish poets. Burns is as far above Ramsay and Fergusson and the Sempills of Beltrees as Dunbar—who had the same instinct for veracity—is above the other Scottish Makars. And I am quite willing to admit that I myself consider this intellectual power, this instinct for veracity, the most significant single element in the "irresistibly attractive" personality of the Ayrshire farmer who became the most distinguished of Scotland's many distinguished sons.

II

His Reputation

IN discussing Burns's reputation, I have in mind a distinctly broader definition of that term than a precisian might admit. "*Reputation;* credit, honour, character of good", says Dr. Johnson; "'Reputation is an idle and most false imposition; oft got without merit, and lost without deserving'. 'At every word a reputation dies.'" It will be of interest to see what was Burns's "character of good", according to various critics and biographers who have pictured him. But of at least equal significance will be the reception accorded his poetry during the hundred and fifty years that have elapsed since the publication of his first volume. Even before Burns's death these two matters had become intimately involved with one another. People who disapproved of Burns's conduct were loath to praise his poetry; those who were offended by his verse, pointed derisively at flaws in his character; those who delighted in his poems, apologized for unfortunate incidents in his career. Much of his best work, moreover, grows so immediately out of his own experiences, that even if the confusion had not been of long standing, it would still be difficult to separate the reputation of the man from that of his poetry. Hawthorne came close to the truth when he wrote, in 1860, that there was no other writer "whose life as a man has so much to do with his fame, and throws such a necessary light upon whatever he has produced". Consequently I shall make no attempt at this time to unravel the twisted cord, but shall consider the man and his works as a single phenomenon in the history of English literature, and shall try to point out how this phenomenon has been viewed at different times and in different places.

What Burns's reputation is to-day, we all know. Would it be an overstatement to say that he enjoys the affection and admiration of a widerspread and more numerous body of cultivated readers than any other of our chief English poets? Such generalizations are always dangerous and usually unnecessary; but in this instance I feel justified in risking the assertion. Who can challenge his primacy on this joint score of affection for the man and admiration for his work? Even the most partisan of his admirers would admit that he does not belong in the inner circle of the world's greatest poets; they would concede the justice of Walt Whitman's statement that Burns's place is "near, but outside the mighty temple of the Gods of song and art". No one to-day links his name with Shakespeare's, as his eulogists were inclined to do not long ago. Chaucer accomplished more than Burns in the field of narrative poetry;

HIS REPUTATION 43

Browning's analyses of human character are more subtle than Burns's; Wordsworth, brooding over the commonplace mysteries of life, gives us more than Burns of intellectual stimulus movingly blended with emotional satisfaction. But there is an aloofness, an austerity, about certain of the greatest poets which erects an almost impenetrable barrier between them and the generality of their readers. Lord Grey phrased the matter well in one of the essays written towards the close of his life, when he said this of Shakespeare:

> When I went out of office after eleven years of it, very tired, and for the time not fit for anything, I spent some weeks alone in the country. During that time I read, or re-read, several of Shakespeare's plays. The impression produced upon me by his incredible power and range was really that of awe; I felt almost afraid to be in the same room with him—as if I were in the presence of something supernatural.

There is none of that quality about Burns. The better one knows him, the more one wants "to be in the same room with him"; to hear the tones of his voice; to look into the eyes that Scott saw and remembered. "They glowed," said Sir Walter; "yes, I say positively glowed." And joined to this affection for the man is admiration for his utterly unique accomplishment in poetry. As a result of this two-fold appeal Burns enjoys a popularity that is hardly credible. For twenty-five years I have had the pleasure of lecturing on English literature to American university students, and have yet to find anyone as certain as Burns to awaken their interest. I have seen luckless men in the reading rooms of the Chicago Public Library, seeking warmth and shelter from the chill of winter, and scanning in vain the "Help Wanted" columns of the daily papers. And I have seen these same men, baffled and disheartened, call for Burns's poems, to read and read again the well-worn pages, till ten o'clock brought closing time, and sent these humble admirers of Burns out into the night. I have found the scholars of to-day so interested in Burns that a bibliography listing the publications of only the past decade would include some nine biographical studies, at least fifteen editions of his prose or verse, and over a hundred miscellaneous articles. Yes, Burns's position to-day is well established. He is esteemed and beloved in a significantly unique fashion.

It would require a large volume to set forth in detail the history of Burns's reputation, thus broadly interpreted, and to show the various steps by which this astonishing popularity has been built up. If this volume should ever be written, it would present a record which might be briefly summarized thus:

The 1786 Kilmarnock edition raised Burns from the position of a village rhymester to that of

"Ayrshire's bard"; the 1787 Edinburgh edition made him known and admired far beyond the limits of Scotland. But after the first enthusiasm had spent itself—an enthusiasm which Burns realized was occasioned in part by the novelty of his situation—Burns was allowed to step off the stage into something approximating retirement at Ellisland and Dumfries. His death in 1796 revived interest in him and his work; various obituary notices suggested that he had drunk himself to death, and prepared scandal-loving readers for Heron's biography, which, in 1797, blackened his personal reputation as enthusiastically as it praised his poetry. The subscription set on foot for Burns's family, and the publicity attendant upon the preparation of a collected edition of Burns's works, kept his name before the public till 1800, when Dr. Currie's four-volume *Works of Robert Burns, with an Account of his Life*, attracted attention throughout the English-speaking world. Cromek's *Reliques of Robert Burns* (1808), with the reviews by Jeffrey and Scott, and Lockhart's biography (1828), with Carlyle's incisive review, established Burns's position as one of the significant figures in English literature,—a man to be pitied for his misfortunes and condemned for his misconduct, but honoured for his accomplishment. Then in 1834 came Allan Cunningham's elaborate eight-volume edition and readable biography, a work that was to equal Currie's in popularity, and to foist upon an uncritical public a considerable amount of imaginative mendacity disguised as sober fact.

The next twenty-five years were to see editions of Burns's works on the lists of many publishing houses in Great Britain and America, and on those of a few in France and Germany. His name appeared often in the periodicals, particularly in America, where an occasional writer seemed puzzled and annoyed by the fact that such a dissipated wastrel as Burns was supposed to have been, could have written such admirable verse. In 1859, the centenary of his birth, his admirers rose to his defence; a chorus of *ex parte* pleas all but drowned the voices of more temperate critics. Then, as memories of the anniversary eloquence grew dimmer, Burns again passed from public attention. The years from 1860 to 1895 saw him not actually in eclipse, but distinctly less prominent than he had been from, say, 1828 to 1855. His position as a writer seemed definitely established; his character, too, was no longer a matter for debate. Everything that was worth knowing about him had apparently been discovered.

Then came 1896, the hundredth anniversary of Burns's death, bringing the great Glasgow Exhibition, William Wallace's revision of Chambers's *Life and Works of Robert Burns*, and the Henley-

Henderson edition of his poetry. This last showed what results might be attained when a scholar like T. F. Henderson set himself to the task of constructing a reliable text of Burns's verse, and a critic like Henley undertook to winnow out verifiable fact from the mass of legend and gossip that had grown up around his name. Once again there seemed little left for critic or scholar to do.

But during the forty years since the hundredth anniversary celebrations, so much has been accomplished towards the determination of the text of Burns's prose, a knowledge of the facts of his life, and an understanding of his character, that Henley and Henderson appear to have been only pioneers in the attempt to learn and tell the whole truth about Burns. Professor Ferguson's edition of the letters has taken its place beside the Centenary edition of the poems; various biographical studies and pertinent articles in the *Burns Chronicle* have cleared up perplexing uncertainties in Burns's career; two distinguished physicians, Dr. Harry B. Anderson of Toronto and Sir James Crichton-Browne of Dumfries, have given us the true explanation of his early death, and have definitely exploded the old canard that he fell a victim to syphillis and alcoholism. The temper of the criticism published during these four decades has been far more judicial than that of seventy-five years ago. There is no longer any excuse for hysterical apology to counterbalance malicious gossip. Modern scholarship has come close to giving us a picture of the man in his habit as he lived. The more we have learned that is indisputably true, the greater has become our admiration for the Burns who is only now emerging from the storm-clouds and mists of a century and a half. His popularity with readers of all classes continues undimmed from year to year; his "character of good" is more certainly established than it has ever been in the past. As never before we realize that his reputation was not got without merit, and cannot be lost without deserving.

Something like that—in barest outline—has been the history of Burns's reputation. Now, making those *exclusiones debitae naturae* which Pater advised, I propose to look in greater detail at certain typical sections of the story as a whole, certain pages from this unwritten volume.

For example, early in his career Burns was conscious that he had enemies as well as friends. The *Epistle to J. Lapraik*, entered in Burns's first Commonplace Book on June 1, 1785, over a year before the Kilmarnock volume appeared, is a vigorous, off-hand exposition of what one might call the youthful poet's attitude towards things in general. It was not written for publication; it has all the earmarks of a genuine and possibly thoughtless sincerity. Stanza XVI runs thus:

> I winna blaw about mysel,
> As ill I like my fauts to tell;
> But friends, an' folk that wish me well,
>   They sometimes roose me;
> Tho', I maun own, as monie still
>   As far abuse me.

By the time these lines were written, Burns had lived through the sorry episode of his father's bankruptcy, had earned a local notoriety because of his affair with Elizabeth Paton, and had given some offence by circulating satiric verses in manuscript. Already tongues were wagging; the unco' guid had him marked as a bad lot, and he was well aware of their opinion.

Four years later a sentence in a letter to John Logan shows that in one way or another he had added generously to the number of his ill-wishers. "I have enemies enow, God knows," wrote Burns, "tho' I do not wantonly add to the number." Not "wantonly", perhaps, but none the less successfully, Burns offended many of his contemporaries. In Irish parlance, "he had a tongue in his head". He was the most brilliant talker in Scotland, and he talked wherever there was a listener. To differ from him on politics or religion or social philosophy was to invite his ridicule; to patronize him, or to wear the cloak of the hypocrite, was to open the flood-gates of his wrath; fortunate the man who escaped with merely a verbal lashing, and was not raised to a bad eminence by written verse. And of course the people whom he offended "talked back"; ineffectively, to be sure, but persistently. Thus at the very beginning of his career Burns experienced what was to be his lot almost to the present: enthusiastic praise and harsh criticism, in both of which politics, personalities, and poetry were thoroughly intermingled.

Not all of Burns's enemies contented themselves with muttered imprecation or whispered gossip. A picturesque and crabbed Tarbolton tailor, Alexander Tait, whom Burns knew during the years at Lochlie, undertook to pay Burns in coin of his own stamp—just why, one can hardly tell, though Burns's theological views might well have given offence to Tait's Auld Licht conservatism. Then too, it was hard for Tait to be friendly with anyone who was writing verse, for he himself aspired to the laureateship of Tarbolton parish. Harmless David Sillar once felt the lash of Tait's displeasure, expressed in lines beginning with the astonishing couplet,

> My pipe wi' wind I maun gae fill 'er
> And play a tune to Davie Sillar.

Several times Tait launched his doggerel shafts against Burns; once, apparently, in retaliation for some rhyme that Burns had set afloat concerning Saunders himself. Whatever song Burns may have made on Tait seems to be lost; but the reply remains, with its characteristic opening stanza:

> Now I maun trace his pedigree
> Because he made a sang on me,
> And let the world look and see
> Just wi' my tongue
> How Rab and Clootie did agree
> When he was young.

When William Burnes, father of the poet, was in trouble with McLure, landlord of Lochlie, and the sheriff's officer "sequestrated" his stock and crops, Saunders Tait was an interested observer, and wrote his account of the episode with spiteful zest. But it was Burns's propensity for involving himself in amatory difficulties that gave Tait the opportunity for his most devastating stanzas. No detail seems to have escaped him; with ribald glee he followed Burns through his experiences, and grew positively ecstatic in recounting Jean Armour's misfortunes.

Burns himself gave little heed to Tait's ill-natured verses; not even a passing allusion to him appears in Burns's correspondence. Apparently other people had the same slight regard for him; for in 1790, when Saunders followed Burns's example and published a volume of poems, the venture fell flat. The disappointed scribbler, chagrined at his failure, vented his spleen upon himself by gathering in all the copies he could lay hands on and—so tradition has it—destroying them. Only one seems to have escaped the fire. Whoever finds himself within the hospitable walls of the Mitchell Library in Glasgow will do well to ask for a sight of the unique copy of Tait's *Poems and Songs,* published probably in Paisley; for in it he will see first-hand evidence of what Scottish vernacular poetry can be at its worst, and of the hostility that Burns aroused when fame was first coming to him.

Burns's first two publications would inevitably have brought him into disfavour with the orthodox, even if his personal conduct had been quite exemplary. To list many instances in which Burns was the victim of what we might call ecclesiastical disapprobation, would be a work of supererogation. But four examples, spread over a hundred years, will give a fair idea of how persistent the pietists have been in their attempts to counteract Burns's growing popularity. The record does not show how many verbal assaults Burns—or Burns's memory—had to endure; knowing the acrimony of theological disputation, however, one may be sure that many a Kirk Session considered his lamentable influence. Not infrequently the wrath of his moralizing critics flamed from the printed page; a number of these documents are still in existence, to amuse and delight whoever cares to read them.

For example, hardly was the 1787 Edinburgh edition off the press when an unnamed critic attacked Burns in a chap-book preserved in the British Museum: "On reading Burns's poems", wrote the outraged protestor,

> and some other productions in his defence, my feelings have been so shocked, that I should think it criminal not to contribute with the virtuous few who have already appeared on the side of injur'd truth.—It is certainly a very agreeable article of licentious faith, that although led astray by fierce passions and wild pleasures, yet 'the light that lead astray is light from heaven.' . . . Such articles, together with the contaminating spirit that runs through this work, are calculated to do more injury to religion, and virtue, than all the atheistical, deistical, and heretical books that have been written this last century.

Following this preliminary blast appears a parody of *To a Daisy*—the whole thing done in such fashion that I suspect a feminine authorship for the pamphlet.

The Reverend William Peebles, of Newtown-on-Ayr, was another who found it impossible to approve of Burns. He read *The Holy Fair* when it first appeared, and discovered that it was highly offensive; for he was a staunch supporter of Auld Licht dogma and practice. One stanza in particular rankled:

> In guid time comes an antidote
> Against sic poison'd nostrum;

> For Peebles, frae the water-fit,
>   Ascends the holy rostrum:
> See, up he's got the word o' God,
>   An' meek an' mim has view'd it,
> While Common-sense has ta'en the road,
>   An' aff, an' up the Cowgate
>   Fast, fast that day.

For precisely twenty-five years Peebles nursed his wrath to keep it warm. Then, in 1811, when Burns's tongue and pen, silent in St. Michael's Kirkyard for fifteen years, were no longer to be feared, Peebles published his reply: *Burnomania: The Celebrity of Robert Burns considered in a Discourse Addressed to all Real Christians*. *The Holy Fair* and *Tam o' Shanter* are destructive of public morals, said the good doctor; let us have done with this adulation of their author! Could there be better testimony to Burns's reputation in 1811 than that?

Criticism of this sort appeared in America as well as in Scotland. In 1848 Samuel Tyler, a Baltimore lawyer, published an astonishing volume called *Robert Burns: As a Poet, and as a Man* (New York, 1848), a superlative example of the rhapsodic eulogy provoked by the attacks of the moralists. The book found its way to the offices of the *Biblical Repertory and Princeton Review*, where it was looked upon with Presbyterian disfavour. "The author fails to carry our convictions by his ingenious reasonings or pleadings", wrote the reviewer in April, 1849;

> we enter our dissent not only as a matter of literary judgment, but with something approaching to moral disapprobation. . . . We fear that [Mr. Tyler's] admiration of the poet has seduced him into an undue approbation of the man; or rather, perhaps, into excessive lenity in handling the notorious vices of his private life. This, however, is a topic for the discussion of which we have neither the time nor the taste.

Poor Burns! The conservative tradition was strong at Princeton, where, eighty-five years ago, Daddy Auld and Black Russell would have found congenial spirits.

Thirty years later the "Orthodox, orthodox, Wha believe in John Knox", were still keen on the scent. In 1880 the English Society for Promoting Christian Knowledge published a work by W. H. D. Adams entitled *Wrecked Lives, or, Men who have Failed.* Burns is one of the luckless wrecks whose reputations dangle in chains from the gibbet of Christian disapproval. So unrelenting has been the opposition of a certain type of ecclesiastic to "rantin', rovin', Robin".

On the other side of the ledger, indicative of the enthusiasm aroused by Burns's first two volumes, one finds such testimony as that furnished by the rapid and widespread reprinting of the 1787 Edinburgh edition. (Most of the facts have been several times set forth, but it will not be amiss to review them for the light they throw on Burns's reputation.) The volume, a subscription edition, appeared in Edinburgh soon after the middle of April, 1787. It was printed by William Smellie, whom Burns affectionately called "that old veteran in genius, wit, and baudry"; bound by Scot; and published, in so far as there was a publisher other than Burns himself, by William Creech, the owner of the copyright. Almost at once Strahan and Cadell, with whom Creech had a close connection, brought it out in London as a trade venture. On July 7, John Reid, bookseller and stationer of New York, advertised it for sale in the columns of the New York *Independent Journal*, sandwiching it between announcements of Seneca's *Morals* and Bruce's *Memoirs*.[1] Early in 1788 the volume was reprinted—piratically, of course—in Philadelphia, which thus won the honour of being the first city outside the British Isles to publish Burns's work. The announcement of this edition stated that a number of the poems had already appeared in American periodicals. Later in 1788 another reprint came out in New York; 1789 saw pirated editions issued in Belfast and Dublin. Thus within two years after the first publication in Edinburgh, editions had come out in London,

---

[1] Anna M. Painter, "American Editions of the Poems of Burns before 1800" (*The Library*, London, 1932, p. 434).

Philadelphia, New York, Belfast, and Dublin. By 1791 the volume was at least known in Germany; in that year Burns's name is included in J. D. Reuss's *Das Gelehrte England: oder, Lexicon der jetzt-lebenden Schriftsteller*.[2] Such facts indicate a far wider and more rapid spread of Burns's reputation than is, perhaps, generally recognized. Clearly enough, this Edinburgh edition brought him fame in a measure denied to most youthful poets.

Had the volume attracted no attention outside Scotland, there would still be good evidence of Burns's popularity at home in the long list of imitations which were to see the light—temporarily, at least—within a few years after Burns had achieved his success. Reviewers were singing Burns's praises; though he himself seems to have paid scant attention to their comments, for he never alludes to them in his letters, other people read them, and tried as they could to gain similar applause. Burns was aware of what was going on; once or twice he helped a rhyming correspondent polish a verse or launch a volume. But though he may have been flattered by the attempts at imitation, he apparently rated the products at approximately their true worth. A casual remark in a letter to Mrs. Dunlop is eloquent in its vivid phraseology: "My success has encouraged such a

[2] W. Macintosh, *Burns in Germany* (Aberdeen, 1928), p. 31.

shoal of ill-spawned monsters to crawl into public notice, under the title of Scots Poets, that the very term Scots Poetry borders on the burlesque." This was written on March 4, 1789, when only the fore-runners of the shoal had made their appearance; but already there were enough of them and to spare. William Taylor of Currie hurried his *Scots Poems* off the press in Edinburgh before the close of 1787; the year 1788 brought similar volumes from Burns's friend John Lapraik, from James Macaulay, and Gavin Turnbull, and an anonymous work bearing the picturesquely descriptive title *Poetical Dialogues on Religion, in the Scots Dialect, between two Gentlemen and two Ploughmen.*

By 1789 Davie Sillar, Burns's former neighbour in Tarbolton parish, had accumulated enough manuscript "to mak a buik", and John Wilson, who had printed Burns's Kilmarnock volume, was entrusted with the task of bringing it out. As if there would be virtue in the very type used for the *Address to the Deil* and *The Cotter's Saturday Night*, Sillar ordered his work set from the same font, and even specified an exact reproduction of Burns's title page—*mutatis mutandis*—border ornaments and all. Wilson had a flair for good printing, and produced an attractive volume which, from a distance of ten feet, makes as good an impression as Burns's. But when one begins to read, one realizes that more is needed than excellent press-work and the Scottish dialect to ensure the life of a poem.

The next six years saw a copious outpouring of similar futilities. Fisher, Morison, Sherrifs, Mylne, Tait, Learmont, Little,—"Janet Little, the Scotch Milkmaid"—Galloway, Graham,—the Reverend James Graham, who went Burns one better by publishing verse in English, Scots, and Latin—Farquhar, Lauderdale,—even their names are forgotten except by bibliographers. But the fact that they tried as they could to follow Burns's example is good evidence of his reputation at the time.

To such a statement one obvious objection might be made. "How do you know", a critic might say, "that these publications of Scottish verse were inspired by Burns's success? Were not these forgotten writers merely conforming to a well-established tradition in thus adding their contributions to the large mass of eighteenth-century vernacular literature? Even if Burns had never written a line, is it not probable that most of them would have published *Poems Chiefly in the Scottish Dialect*"?

The question is a fair one; the attempt to answer it involves one in a study of Scottish poetry during, say, the half-century preceding the appearance of the Kilmarnock volume. It is true that Ramsay, who virtually re-established the vernacular as a literary dialect, and Fergusson, who showed what might be accomplished with it, seem in retrospect to have occupied positions of such eminence as would have made them powerful influences on national fashions in literature. But I wonder whether Burns, who freely acknowledged his debt to these two predecessors, was not relatively alone in recognizing their examples as worthy of emulation. An examination of the notable collection of Scottish poetry in the Mitchell Library discloses little vernacular poetry written between Ramsay and Burns. That there was a demand for reprints of what might be called the classics of old Scottish literature is proved by such publications as *Ancient Scottish Poems*, Barbour's *Bruce*, Ballantine's *Vertue and Vyce*, *The Gude and Godlie Ballades*, Gavin Douglas's *Aeneid*, Dunbar's *Thistle and the Rose*, Montgomery's *Cherry and the Slae*, *Christ's Kirk on the Green*, and others of the same sort. During these decades there also appeared several collections of English and Scottish songs, like *The Charmer* (Edinburgh, 1751); *The Goldfinch* (Edinburgh, 1777); *The Lark* (Perth, 1775); and *The Nightingale* (Edinburgh, 1776). These fugitive volumes contained a mass of old and recent lyrics, some of which were in Scots. Obviously the tradition of a vernacular song literature was well established at the time. But of vernacular poetry, as differentiated from the popular songs, the period produced little. Blacklock, who in 1785 was honoured as the foremost living Scottish poet, seems never to have published a line in Scots. Michael Bruce, whose poetic remains Burns helped print for the benefit of his family, wrote in English. Except for Fergusson's dialect poems, the characteristic poetry of the entire period shows the strong influence of English standards, and hardly suggests the existence of a native tradition. Symbolically enough, Fergusson's grave in the Canongate Kirkyard was unmarked, till Burns erected a stone over it. What eighteenth-century Scotland considered poetry, before Burns showed the way to something better, may be gathered from such works as Robert Alves's *Time, an Elegy* (Aberdeen, 1766); or A. Bushe's *Socrates, a Dramatic Poem* (Port Glasgow, 1762); or Robert Colvill's *The Fate of Julia, an Elegiac Poem* (Edinburgh, 1769); or Alexander Cuthbertson's *Elegy on T. and A. Wardrop* (Glasgow, 1764); or David Dickson's *True Christian Love* (Glasgow, 1764); or Ralph Erskine's *New Version of the Song of Solomon* (Glasgow, 1752); or David Fisher's *The Independent Faith Displayed* (Edinburgh, 1775); or, at its picturesque worst, from any of the voluminous outpourings of James Maxwell, who signed himself "Poet in Paisley", and sometimes added the initials S.D.P., which he interpreted as meaning "Student of Divine Poetry".

The fact has never been sufficiently emphasized that Burns's choice of Scots as a vehicle for poetry was, in 1785, a revolutionary step—almost as revolutionary as Milton's choice of English for his contribution to a volume of Greek and Latin elegies on Edward King. And when one finds the current of eighteenth-century Scottish poetry running steadily in the direction of the English tradition till Burns's work appeared, and then as suddenly reversing itself, one is justified in concluding that it was Burns's example which occasioned the change, and in asserting that this fact throws an interesting light on his reputation and popularity at that time.

But Burns had not long to enjoy the fame his publications brought him, for in just ten days less than ten years after the appearance of the Kilmarnock volume, he was dead, and was spared the pain of reading the obituary notices in Edinburgh and London journals. When he died, he was one of Dumfries's most honoured citizens. He was maintaining his large family in comfortable independence; he was a freeman of the town, enjoying the full privileges of the burgess-ship conferred on him in June of 1787; he was an honorary member of the Dumfries library, which he had helped to establish; he was one of the organizers of the Royal Volunteers, and had been for some months a member of the small governing committee of that corps; he had been acting supervisor of the Dumfries excise district, and was making an admirable record in the service; his long list of friends included men like Gray and White of the Academy faculty, David Staig, for twenty years provost of the burgh, and Colonel Arent de Peyster, commandant of the volunteers. The elaborate pageantry of Burns's funeral was an attempt on the part of all Dumfries to demonstrate the affection and admiration which he had inspired.

The newspapers at once took cognizance of Burns's death. A paragraph in the Edinburgh *Evening Courant* of July 23—from where it was copied into several other journals—was the work of George Thomson, publisher of the *Select Scotish Airs*, for whom Burns was serving as unpaid and overworked editor. Thomson praised Burns's poetry in conventional journalistic fashion, but added a damning sentence concerning his character: "The public, to whose amusement he has so largely contributed, will learn with regret that his extraordinary endowments were accompanied with frailties which rendered them useless to himself and his family." This statement—which Burns's friends in Dumfries quite properly resented—Thomson elaborated upon in the much longer *Memoirs of the Late Robert Burns, the Scotch Poet*, which he prepared for the *London Chronicle* of

July 29-31.³ In the eight hundred words of this article Thomson painted Burns's character in black enough colours:

> His nights were devoted to books and the muse, except when they were wasted in those haunts of village festivity, and in the indulgences of the social bowl, to which the Poet was but too immoderately attached in every period of his life.... He was not qualified to fill a superior station to that which was assigned him [as an exciseman]. We know that his manners refused to partake the polish of genteel society, that his talents were often obscured and finally impaired by excess.... His conduct and his fate afford but too melancholy proofs [of the failings of genius].⁴

In estimating the value of Thomson's testimony as to Burns's character, one should remember that Thomson had never met Burns, that he had never visited Dumfries, and that his second-hand information concerning Burns's career was so inaccurate that in this "memoir" he referred to Burns's first publication as "a coarse edition of his poems . . . published at Dumfries".⁵

Why Thomson felt impelled thus gratuitously to besmirch the character of the man who was

---

³Professor J. DeL. Ferguson, in "The Earliest Obituary of Burns" (*Modern Philology*, vol. XXXII, p. 179, Nov., 1934), was the first to show Thomson's authorship of the *Chronicle* article. The evidence he adduces, though lacking the definiteness of absolute proof, is convincingly strong.

⁴Quoted by Ferguson, *op. cit.*, p. 180.

⁵Quoted by Ferguson, *ibid.*

"bearing the burden" of his *Select Scotish Airs*, one cannot even guess. Burns had given him *Highland Mary* and *Duncan Gray* and *Scots Wha Hae* and *Auld Lang Syne* and *A Man's a Man for a' That* and fifty other songs to boot, and on his death-bed had apologized for not having been able to do more! In return, Thomson tried to swindle him as he lay dying, and within a week of his funeral called him a drunken reprobate, unfit for the society of decent people.

If Thomson's article had been once published and then forgotten, the story would have been bad enough. But unfortunately it was "reprinted in full in the *Gentleman's Magazine* for August, 1796, and abridged in the *Monthly Magazine and British Register* for the same month".[6] Thus put into circulation under the aegis of the *Gentleman's*, this libellous sketch of Burns took rank as an authentic portrait, and Burns became known not as he was, but as a vicious, scandal-mongering imagination had pictured him. "Damned illiberal lies" Burns's friend Syme called Thomson's work; "illiberal" seems a charitable adjective.

I have been thus particular concerning Thomson's memoir because, as Professor Ferguson has pointed out, it was this document that gave Heron and Currie their cues for the earliest biographies of Burns. By the time these two had done their

[6]Ferguson, *ibid.*

work, Burns's personal reputation had been established, and the poor poet had scarcely a tattered rag left of his "character of good". The portrait thus painted was to be challenged, to be sure, on the score of its accuracy; but never effectively, I believe, till within the past ten years.

But even while Burns's character was suffering in this fashion, the merit of his poems was becoming clear to a constantly widening circle of readers. The fact that the *Gentleman's Magazine* thought him worthy of space is indicative of the attention his poems had aroused in England. Lamb and Coleridge and Wordsworth, as one might have expected, were reading him with enthusiasm. Shortly after Burns's death Coleridge sent Lamb the lines *To a Friend*; one brief section shows Coleridge's opinion of Burns so clearly that it is worth quoting:

> Is thy Burns dead?
> And shall he die unwept, and sink to earth
> "Without the meed of one melodious tear?"
> Thy Burns, and Nature's own beloved bard,
> Who to the "Illustrious of his native land
> So properly did look for patronage."[7]
> Ghost of Maecenas! hide thy blushing face!
> They snatched him from the sickle and the plough
> To gauge ale-firkins.

Such a passage might indicate nothing more

[7]Slightly misquoted from the Preface to Burns's 1787 edition.

than a personal admiration for Burns on the part of Coleridge and Lamb. But the Royal Literary Fund, established at London, would not have contributed to any subscription for Burns's family had the managers not considered him a figure of national importance. Hence it is significant that on October 20, 1796, the Fund voted "That Twenty five Pounds be sent to the Committee appointed to collect Subscriptions for the benefit of the Widow and Children of the late Robert Burns".[8] Five years later the Fund made a supplementary grant of twenty pounds, good evidence that their approval of Burns had not been affected by what Heron and Currie had said of him.

It would be interesting to learn what English and Scottish university men thought of Burns at this time, but unfortunately I have at the present little information on this point. What evidence there is, suggests that he was being read with appreciation. For instance, in the summer of 1803 the Reverend Philip Homer, under-master of Rugby and Fellow of Magdelen, visited Dumfries on his way to the western highlands. In his *Observations*, published in London the following year, he commented on the condition of Burns's grave, and added this remark: "His fame is independent of [his fellow townsmen's] exertions,

[8] J. C. E[wing], "The Literary Fund and Robert Burns" (*Burns Chronicle*, 1934, p. 70).

and posterity will do him the most ample justice, however his remains may be neglected by the inhabitants of Dumfries."[9]

It was also in the summer of 1803 that another English university graduate, in the company of his sister, stood beside Burns's grave and mused on

> Him who walked in glory and in joy
> Following his plough, along the mountain-side.[10]

The poetic results of Wordsworth's visit to Dumfries are well-known: the stanzas *At the Grave of Burns*, and *Thoughts Suggested the Day Following*, both genuinely moving comments on Burns's accomplishment and Wordsworth's indebtedness to him, and the lines *To the Sons of Burns*, rather wishy-washy moralizing on the dangers of bad company and strong drink. I often wonder why Wordsworth included the third in his next publication, the *Poems in Two Volumes* of 1807, but hid the first two in his desk drawer till 1845. Was Wordsworth's own affair with Annette Vallon too fresh in his memory to permit public eulogy of one who—unlike Wordsworth—never concealed his misdeeds? Or was he temperamentally averse to committing himself on such a controversial matter

[9] Quoted by J. Gibson, *Bibilography of Robert Burns*, (Kilmarnock, 1881), p. 125.
[10] Wordsworth was reading Burns at least as early as 1787. See a letter by Dorothy Wordsworth, Dec. 17, 1787, in the *Early Letters of William and Dorothy Wordsworth* (Oxford, 1935), p. 12.

as Burns's reputation? In 1816 he publicly entered the lists in Burns's defence, and published his *Letter to a Friend of Robert Burns* (James Gray), which he apparently intended to be a corrective for the current misinterpretation of Burns's character. But unfortunately Jeffrey's review of the *Excursion*, that withering review beginning "This will never do", was fresh in Wordsworth's mind; and he seems to have been more eager to repay Jeffrey than to clear Burns's name. The impression left by the pamphlet is not over-creditable to its author. Two years later Hazlitt, in the seventh of his *Lectures on the English Poets*, took Wordsworth to task for his faint praise of Burns, and promised to say something concerning his position in English literature. But Hazlitt, with characteristic fondness for the tangential, wandered far afield, and gave his auditors little to ponder over except the statement that Burns's poetry is "a very highly sublimated essence of animal existence".

It would be a pleasant task to follow Burns's progress through the pages of English criticism, and to discuss such well-known interpretations— or misinterpretations—as those of Carlyle, Arnold, Stevenson, and Henley. But keeping in mind my hope to place an old idea in a somewhat new light, I turn away from these familiar matters to comment briefly on the Burns festivals of 1844 and

1859, and on Burns's reputation in Germany, France, and the United States.

The year 1844 saw a notable commemoration on the anniversary of Burns's death. The curious can read Thomas Aird's account in *Blackwood's*, or Douglas Jerrold's "Scotland Repentant" in *Punch*; Burns himself would certainly have enjoyed the latter. A thousand people crowded a pavilion at Ayr, and paid fifteen shillings each for a lunch that Jerrold described as consisting of "cold tongue, a plate of gooseberries almost ripe, and some mystery calling itself sherry". Burns's sons were present, and his daughter, with her daughters; the Earl of Eglinton provided food and drink for all who could not afford the collation; and not even the deluge of rain interfered with the patriotic enthusiasm engendered by the occasion. The editor of *Punch* found something amusing about it all, and also something inexplicable; for as a Sassenach he was estopped from really understanding Burns. And I do not believe I am reading too intently between the lines when I suspect Jerrold of being a little envious of these Ayrshiremen who claimed Burns as one of their "ain folk". Be that as it may, the 1844 celebration speaks eloquently for Burns's hold on the affections of his countrymen.

In 1859, the centenary of Burns's birth, enthusiasm rose to such a pitch that the number of recorded celebrations reached the astonishing total of eight hundred and seventy-two. Whiskey flowed and haggis steamed from Alloway to Calcutta and back again. "'Twad be owre lang a tale to tell" to say much about these demonstrations; but two of the gatherings merit a passing word. At Boston, General John S. Tyler occupied the chair; Emerson, Holmes, Lowell, and Whittier were among the persons who made it clear that American admiration for the poet was genuine and intelligent. Incidentally, I doubt whether a more distinguished list of participants could have been found at many of the eight hundred and seventy-one other dinners. Most notable of all the commemorations, however, from the point of view of public interest, was that held on January 25 at the Crystal Palace, London. Several months before, the managers had offered a prize of fifty guineas for the best poem in honour of Burns; over six hundred manuscripts were submitted. On the night of January 25, when the winner was to be named, *Punch* again sent its editor, this time the great Shirley Brooks himself, to "cover" the meeting. To judge by his accounts,[11] all London except a few luckless cabmen packed the auditorium, and listened enwrapt while the chosen poem, not by Tennyson, or Browning, or Landor, but by Mrs. Isa Craig Knox, who had been born in Edinburgh, was declaimed from the rostrum. When the

[11]*Punch*, Jan. 29, Feb. 5, 1859.

exercises were over, and the crowd had fought its way out into the streets, Mr. Punch betook himself to a public house to meditate on the affair over a glass of stout. It is all amusing enough, as Brooks tells the story, once in verse suggestive of *Evangeline*, just then at the height of its popularity, and once in rhyme. The celebration as a whole was not, perhaps, in the best of taste. But I wonder whether there is any other English poet in whose honour such a gathering could have been held; and whether, after all allowances have been made, it was not convincing indication of Burns's popularity with the great mass of the English reading public.

Yet even in this year of jubilee the old note of hostility reappears. An anonymous pamphlet, published at Glasgow, bears the title *Burns' Centenary. Are such honours due to the Ayrshire Bard*, and presents to the reader this query: "To the lovers of their country, who desire to see temperance, virtue, and frugality blessing its teeming millions, we would say, pause and reflect! Are these to be learned from the life or writings of the man whom you delight to honour?"[12]

German interest in Burns dates, as we have seen, from at least as early as 1791. But during the next forty years Germany, in the full flush of her greatest creative period, seems to have paid slight attention to Scottish verse. Goethe, how-

[12] Quoted by Gibson, *Bibliography of Robert Burns*, p. 187.

ever, was reading Burns, and wished his countrymen to share the pleasure he was enjoying. In 1831 a slender volume entitled *Choice of Burns's Poems* was published at Ansbach; four years later Allan Cunningham's edition, with his biography, was reprinted at Leipsic. A sentence from the introduction to this latter shows the importance of Goethe's interest in Burns: "The wish of our late prince poet to usher into Germany one of the first poets of the past century—the Scotch Ploughman Poet, Robert Burns—seemed to us a dear legacy, as it were, to be respected awfully and piously fulfilled."[13] Thus Cunningham's portrait of Burns was introduced to Germany, apparently with the *imprimatur* of Goethe; and the misstatements and misinterpretations of "Honest Allan" were foisted upon a public that had no reason for questioning them. But at least Burns's poetry was interesting German readers.

By 1839 this interest had developed to such an extent that P. Kaufmann brought out the first translation of Burns into German, *Gedichte von Robert Burns, uebersetzt von P. Kaufmann* (Stuttgart u. Tübingen, 1839). The next year saw Julius Heintze publishing a similar volume, which had merit enough to occasion a review by Carlyle in the London *Examiner*.[14] Since then German

[13] Quoted by Macintosh, *Burns in Germany*, p. 26.
[14] Issue of Sept. 29, 1840.

editions and translations of Burns have been frequent.

In one important respect Germany, "learned, indefatigable, deep-thinking Germany", to quote *Sartor*, has virtually led the way to an intelligent understanding of Burns's poetic method. The meticulous studies of Molenaar, Meyerfeld, and Ritter have made available a mass of information concerning Burns's "sources" not otherwise readily accessible. Dr. Ritter's *Quellenstudien zu Robert Burns*, though open to most of the criticisms which such investigations often merit, cannot be overlooked by any serious student of Burns's literary backgrounds. More recently Dr. Hans Hecht has written what I consider distinctly the best brief biography of Burns that has yet been published.[15]

Across the Rhine from Germany a volume of translations, *Morceaux Choisis*,[16] appeared in Paris as early as 1826; in 1843 this was followed by the *Poésies Complètes*.[17] But the Gallic temperament is not as closely akin to the Scottish as is the Germanic; France as a whole has paid little attention to Burns. I say "France as a whole"; for if one Frenchman, Auguste Angellier, had done his work thirty years later, there would have been

[15]*Robert Burns: Leben und Wirken des Schottischen Volksdichters* (Heidelberg, 1919). A translation into English has just been announced (Jan., 1936).

[16]Traduits par James Aytoun et J. B. Mesnard (Paris, 1826).

[17]Traduites de l'Écossais par Léon de Wailly (Paris, 1843).

little need for any further critical or biographical studies of Burns. Even as it was, Angellier, though handicapped by the fact that he wrote before the results of recent investigation had become known, produced such a study of Burns and his world as has yet to be equalled in scope.[18]

An inclusive study of Burns's reputation in foreign lands would lead one far beyond the confines of Germany and France. One can see translations of Burns in Danish, Swedish, and Norwegian, in Dutch, Flemish, African Dutch, and platt-Deutsch, in Bohemian, Hungarian, and Russian, in Scotch Gaelic, Irish Gaelic, and Welsh, in Italian, in Hindustani, and even—as a *tour de force*—in classical Latin. I am not qualified to pass on the merits of many of these indications of Burns's popularity abroad, and hence I venture only two comments. First, the pleasantly unintelligible platt-Deutsch seems to me to come reasonably close to conveying the flavour of Burns's dialect. Second, the sinewy compression, the economy, of Burns's language can hardly be better demonstrated than by placing a verse or two of Scots beside the melodious but polysyllabic Italian equivalent. One is inclined almost to believe in the Tower of Babel when one finds Burns's eight-syllable line

>Sing hey my braw John Highlandman!

[18]*Robert Burns*: *La vie, les oeuvres* (2 vols., Paris, 1893).

transformed into

> Cantate, oh! il mio bravo Giovanni il Montanaro!

The story of Burns's reputation in the United States is a long one, and must be drastically condensed. I have already recounted the early sale and reprinting of the 1787 edition in Philadelphia and New York. It is significant that American publishers and readers showed a similar interest in Currie's four-volume life and works of Burns (1800), and in Cromek's *Reliques of Robert Burns* (1808), both of which were reprinted in Philadelphia within less than a year of their English publication. Ever since that time important items in the Burns bibliography have found a generous welcome in America, where interest in Burns developed as steadily as it did in England.

To turn the pages of representative American journals between, say, 1835 and 1860, is to see the evidence underlying such a statement For example, the first number of the Philadelphia *Public Ledger*, March 25, 1836, carried on its front page an article on Burns, borrowed from the most recent New York *Knickerbocker*. The *Southern Literary Messenger* opened its columns several times to writers who found much to praise in Burns. The *National Magazine* and the *Atlantic* published substantial articles on Burns in early issues; Littel's *Living Age* reprinted English criticism of his work. American editors knew that Burns was of general interest to their readers, who approved of his essentially democratic outlook on life, and treasured *Scots Wha Hae* and *A Man's a Man for A' That* almost as if they had been written in Massachusetts or Virginia.

Much early American criticism is of slight significance except as evidence of Burns's growing popularity; some of it is amusing in its fondness for rhapsodic praise. When William P. Frye once declared, at a Washington Burns Festival, that "the name of Robert Burns, Poet, has been and is dearer to a greater number of hearts than any other save that of Christ", he was only doing his best to make certain that no one should ever outstrip him in praise of Burns. He had forgotten, however, that some years earlier Margaret Fuller, Emerson's transcendental associate in the editorial office of the *Dial*, had established her claims to primacy among Burns's admirers by saying that "since Adam there has been none that approached nearer fitness to stand up before God and angels in the naked majesty of manhood than Robert Burns"—a statement that seems to leave Frye a distinctly poor second.

This note of exaggerated eulogy does not mar the utterances of representative American men of letters, many of whom paid sincere tribute to Burns. Whitman, aspiring to write the poetry of a new democracy, pondered long on Burns's success in setting the soul of Scotland to music, and wrote understandingly about him. Whittier, whose lyric instinct was called to life by hearing a wandering tinker sing Burns's verses, who wrote at least one poem in Scots, and whose *Songs of Labor* mark him as familiar with daily toil such as Burns knew, he too gave Burns no uncertain praise. We may well be grateful to the stern but kindly Quaker for the stanza

> Let those who never erred forget
>   His worth in vain bewailings;
> Sweet soul of song! I own my debt
>   Uncancelled by his failings;

and for having had the insight to call Burns "the truest and sweetest of all who have ever sung of home, and love, and humanity". Longfellow, unofficial laureate of America from 1850 to his death in 1882, bore witness to his affection for Burns in the lines beginning

> I see, amid the fields of Ayr,
> A ploughman, who, in foul or fair
>   Sings at his task
> So clear, we know not if it is
> The laverock's song we hear, or his,
>   Nor care to ask.

One is grateful to Dr. Holmes for his half serious and half whimsical remark that

> Burns ought to have passed ten years of his life,
> or five at least, in America; for those words of his,
> A man's a man for a' that
> show that true American feeling belonged to him as
> much as if he had been born in sight of [Bunker Hill].

One remembers Emerson's address at the Boston commemoration in 1859, and his truthful observation that Burns's use of the vernacular furnishes "the only example in history of a language made classic by the genius of a single man". Hawthorne visited the cottage at Alloway, and said that in 1759 it had sheltered "the germ of the richest human life which mankind then had within its circumference". The American consul at Liverpool went also to Dumfries, and was impressed by the difference between the humble, almost squalid, setting for Burns's last years, and the magnificence of his accomplishment. Thinking of this contrast, he wrote, with characteristic penetration, "There must have been something very grand in his immediate presence, some strangely impressive character in his natural behavior, to have caused him to seem like a demi-god so soon". But perhaps it was Lowell who came nearest to saying what America as a whole wished to have said about Burns. He had never condoned Burns's faults, nor relaxed his own high standards of literary excellence in Burns's favour. At times, indeed, his comments seem unnecessarily harsh. But he made full amends for any possible injustice when he called Burns "a citizen of a country of which we are all citizens, that country of the heart which has no boundaries laid down on the map".

The more I consider this matter of Burns's reputation, the more inclined I am to say that Lowell spoke the truth. For during the past hundred and fifty years Burns, despite ecclesiastical disapprobation and malicious gossip, has come to be loved and admired, for what he was, and for what he wrote, wherever his language can be understood or translations procured. Simple folk of many lands have read him, and have called him brother. Critics have read him, and have praised his accomplishment. Poets have read him, and have borne willing testimony to his enduring worth. And I believe Burns himself would not object if we let a poet have the last word about him in this connection—a Canadian poet, Bliss Carman, whom Burns would have been glad to number among his friends. A single line from one of the *Songs from Vagabondia* says so much that

[19] A friend has just called to my attention—too late for inclusion in the text of this lecture—an interesting comment from the pen of a Chinese scholar. In his volume *My Country and My People* (New York, 1935), Lin Yutang says: "In order to understand China one needs a little detachment and a little simplicity of mind too; that simplicity of mind so well typified by Robert Burns, one of the most Scottish and yet most universal of all poets; who strips our souls bare

there is no need for comment or elaboration. "He loved", says Carman,

> He loved, and made the world his lover.

Anyone of whom that can be said need have little concern about his "character of good".[19]

---

and reveals our common humanity, and the loves and sorrows that common humanity is heir to. Only with that detachment and that simplicity of mind can one understand a foreign nation."

III

His Art

WHOEVER has attended a Burns Club dinner on January 25 remembers the appropriate culmination of the evening's exercises, the toast to "the immortal memory" of him whose birth is commemorated on this day. I suppose many a lover of Burns has risen in response to this toast without realizing the full significance of the phrase. "*Immortal;* exempt from death", says the most famous of all dictionaries. If one stops to think, the phrase takes on a large, almost an awesome meaning; especially from Scottish lips, not given to exaggeration or looseness of speech, it falls with a finality which one rarely associates with mundane affairs or merely human judgments. It assumes that Burns, for one reason or another, will never be forgotten; that so long as men exist they will treasure and honour his memory; that, in this sense, he has already attained an unquestioned exemption from death.

It will be interesting to ask what basis there may be for such an assumption. An attractive personality, no matter how vivid it may have been, will not insure the immortality of Burns's memory. His reputation will fade if based primarily on personal charm, even though that charm still appears between the lines of his printed pages. But if what Burns wrote has been touched by that elixir of eternal life which we name art, then perhaps he may be enrolled among the few whose names the world will not permit to die. For apparently, despite modernistic innovations of the last few decades, the least changeable standards of value that mankind has yet evolved for itself are those of aesthetics. Science and religion have turned their coats many a time in the last twenty-five hundred years; but the things that were beautiful when Pericles set the Parthenon to keep watch over Athens, or the great head of the Sphinx lifted itself above the sands of Egypt—these things are beautiful still, and we remember and honour those who could create them. So, to a friend of Burns, hopeful that his memory will long endure, the most important question is not "What was he like", nor even "What did people say of him after his death", but "How well could he write? Was he a facile rhymester, with a gift for satirizing local celebrities; or was he in some real sense an artist, worthy of that honour which the world bestows upon these creators of enduring beauty?" Only if he was, is there any probability that his memory will be immortal, and that the anniversary toast will not in time seem a piece of ignorance or arrogance. I propose to seek an answer to this question.

In thus committing myself to a discussion of Burns's art, I too, like the chairman who offers the annual toast, am making a large assumption. I assume that we are more or less in agreement as to the meaning of the word *Art*, or at least of the word *Poetry*, since when dealing with Burns we shall be chiefly concerned with the sort of artistic expression which uses verse as its medium. But I realize that this assumption may be unwarranted, and that I might fairly be challenged to define my terms. Were I to be so ordered to "stand and deliver", I should, in good old romantic fashion, knock up the barrel of the pistol with my stout oaken cudgel and decline the issue. One can find definitions of poetry a-plenty, all the way from Aristotle to Carl Sandburg; I do not propose to add another; I shall not enter the lists of aesthetic speculation. I shall try merely to point out certain characteristics of Burns's work which in my judgment, and, I hope, in yours, place the best of it within the category of literary art.

I begin with the smallest thought-unit of a poem, a word. "Words in tuneful order" caught the fancy of the schoolboy who was later to write *Tintern Abbey*, and he gave the rest of his long life to arranging them in patterns that always pleased him and that often pleased his readers. Words, visible, audible symbols of ideas, are the bricks and mortar with which the poet must build his temple of song. Consequently it will be interesting to spend a moment or two scrutinizing Burns's store of words, or, as we call it, his vocabulary.

A philologist would find much of interest in Burns's "word-hoard". Should he examine it in detail, he would discover that, like Scotch whiskey, it is a skilful blend. In it appear elements that belong to standard literary English, others that are common to northern England and lowland Scotland, still others that are pure lowland vernacular, and a few that hail from the Gaelic-speaking highlands. He would point out that Burns's literary language, by which one means his vocabulary woven into the patterns of the printed page, was a language apparently never spoken by anyone, but fabricated by Burns for his particular purposes. He would point out how Burns experimented with the Scottish elements in this language, sometimes adding a little of the vernacular to make a poem more acceptable in its second publication, and sometimes just reversing this process.

Such matters, were they to be discussed by a linguist of parts, would be of interest to all students of Burns. But there are other significant facts concerning his vocabulary which one need not be a philologist to discover. For example, the size of Burns's vocabulary is interesting. One reads in the preface to Reid's concordance to Burns's poetry that the volume contains over 11,400 different words; and I know that not all the words he used in his verse were considered decorous enough for admission to a volume that might be shelved beside Cruden's concordance to the Bible. I know, too, that many words which Burns used in his prose never appeared in his poetry. Consequently I hazard a guess that if ever there should appear a really inclusive concordance of Burns's prose and verse, it would contain possibly 12,500 words. This is, of course, an astonishingly large vocabulary, and compares significantly with Shakespeare's of 24,000 and Milton's of 13,000 words. In the mere size of Burns's vocabulary one discovers an indication of his intellectual power. His mind, teeming with ideas, demanded many words in order that he might have the necessary symbols with which to convey these ideas accurately to his readers. And apparently he never forgot or misused a word that he had come across in his extensive reading.

A second fact that even the amateur philologist will notice is Burns's use of picturesque and skilfully selected verbs. I know few better ways to test a writer's command of his language than to observe his success or failure in the use of verbs, which furnish the bony framework of both poetry and prose. Modifiers, such as adverbs and adjectives, fill in the details; but it is the verbs that really build the idea and present it to the reader. Take eight well-known lines from *Tam* as illustrative of Burns's skill in handling verbs:

> As Tammie glower'd, amaz'd, and curious,
> The mirth and fun grew fast and furious;
> The piper loud and louder blew,
> The dancers quick and quicker flew,
> They reel'd, they set, they cross'd, they cleekit,
> Till ilka carlin swat and reekit,
> And coost her duddies to the wark
> And linket at it in her sark!

This is a slightly unusual passage; but anyone who will read, say, fifty pages of Burns's verse, chosen at random, and will underline all the verbs or verbal derivatives, will see almost at a glance his mastery of these significant parts of speech. And he will realize with a shock of chagrin how flat and insipid is his own language when compared to that of this self-educated farmer.

But, of course, a large and colourful vocabulary is of little use to a poet unless he is skilful in combining words into phrases that have a memorable appropriateness. On this count Burns is not in the same class with Shakespeare, or even with Pope. Nevertheless both his prose and his verse show that his vocabulary was not an inert mass of words lying unused at the bottom of his consciousness. He was not like the golfer who owns a complete outfit of matched woods and irons, but carries only brassie, midiron, and putter; Burns had a full set of clubs, and used them all with ease and precision. Even in his unstudied remarks to intimate friends, and in poems tossed off at hot speed, he showed a notable phrase-making skill.

Give me the pleasure of a few brief quotations to make clear the sort of thing I have in mind. From letters to personal friends, in which Burns was not trying to be "literary", but was merely setting down ideas as they came into his mind, one culls passages like these: to Gavin Hamilton he writes, "My poor unfortunate songs come again across my memory. Damn the pedant, frigid soul of criticism forever and ever"—"Be earnest with that Boanerges of Gospel power, Father Auld, that he will wrestle in prayer for you." To William Cruikshank: "I have fought my way severely through the savage hospitality of this country, the object of all hosts being to send every guest drunk to bed." To Bob Ainslie: "Man is naturally a kind, benevolent animal, but he is dropt into such a damn'd needy situation here in this vexatious world, and has such a whoreson, hungry, growling pack of Necessities, Appetites, Passions, and Desires, about him ready to devour him for want of other food, that in fact he must lay aside his cares for others, that he may look properly to himself." To Alexander Cunningham: "I intend breeding up my eldest boy for the Church; and from an innate dexterity in secret mischief which he possesses, and a certain hypocritical gravity as he looks on the consequences, I have no small hope of him in the sacerdotal line." To James Johnson, publisher of the *Scots Musical Museum:* "I have still a good number of Dr. B's songs, but they take sad hacking and hewing." To Graham of Fintry, who was helping him with the Excise Board: "I don't wish to degrade myself to a hungry rook gaping for a morsel." To John M'Auley: "As I am entered into the holy state of matrimony I trust my face is turned completely Zionward; and as it is a rule with all honest fellows to repeat no grievances, I hope that the little poetic licenses of former days will fall under the oblivious influence of some good-natured statute of celestial prescription." To George Thomson, publisher of the *Select Scotish Airs:* "I give you leave to abuse this song, but do it in the spirit of Christian meekness"; and again, "making a poem is like begetting a son: you cannot know whether you have a wise man or a fool until you produce him to the world and try him." Finally, take this which flashes from a page of the interleaved *Museum:* "[The House of Hanover was] an obscure, beef-witted, insolent race of foreigners whom a conjuncture of circumstances kickt up into power and consequence."

Now no one would even suggest that such picturesque phrases and figures of speech as appear in those random excerpts prove anything concerning the larger and possibly the enduring values of Burns's prose. But, taken in connection with scores of similar passages that might be added to the list, they show the ease and effectiveness with which Burns handled the tools of his trade.

To open the poems in search of similar illustrations of Burns's skill is to find a bewildering richness of material. No reader ever forgets the "screwed-up, grace-proud faces" of *The Holy Fair*, or the "yill-caup commentators"—a phrase that suggests who can say how many overtones and connotations? All the public houses of Scotland and all her centuries of theological disputation form the background of the picture painted by those three words. Or consider the minor memorabilia of *Tam:* a phrase like "nursing her wrath to keep it warm", or the sentence "Tam lo'ed him like a vera brither; They had been fu' for weeks thegither". Possibly the most widely known line in all Burns's work was saved from being lost amid the welter of eighteenth-century pseudo-philosophy by the perfect simplicity of its phrasing: "A man's a man for a' that." But for sheer genius I believe I should choose one line from the "Martial chuck's" song in *The Jolly Beggars*. To see it in its proper setting, it is necessary to place it against the background of the two preceding stanzas:

> The first of my loves was a swaggering blade:
> To rattle the thundering drum was his trade;
> His leg was so tight, and his cheek was so ruddy,
> Transported I was with my sodger laddie.
>
> But the godly old chaplain left him in the lurch;
> The sword I forsook for the sake of the church;
> He risk'd the soul, I ventur'd the body;
> 'Twas then I proved false to my sodger laddie.

And then:

> Full soon I grew sick of my sanctified sot,
> The regiment at large for a husband I got.

It is hard to think of any great English poet, except perhaps Wordsworth or Milton, who—at least secretly—would not have envied Burns the perfection of that "Full soon I grew sick of my sanctified sot"—a line that still hisses with disgust, even though one hundred and fifty years have passed since it was written. Utterly different from these scraps of verse, but equally illustrative of Burns's command of the perfect phrase, is an unexpected pair of lines buried in the mediocrity of *Open the Door to Me, O:*

> The wan moon sets behind the white wave,
> And Time is setting with me, O—

Here the visual image, so simply drawn, is the starting point for a train of reflection that carries the reader far beyond the limits of the picture actually presented. But one need not particularize further. Memorable phrases, testifying to Burns's easy control over his large vocabulary, abound in both his prose and his verse.

Turning, then, from such small units as words, phrases, and single sentences, to certain larger elements in Burns's literary output, one finds much to consider in his prose. As everyone realizes, virtually all of this took the form of letters—easy, familiar letters to his friends and social equals, more formal communications to those above him in rank, and a few "open letters" to the press. All in all we have texts of well over seven hundred of these documents. To read them with attention is to realize that at times Burns could write poor stuff, loaded down with high-flown phraseology that leaves an occasional unpleasant impression of insincerity. As a youth he had sedulously aped the "epistolary style" of Queen Anne's day. The flavour of artificiality acquired during this apprenticeship marred many a page written later in life. But to belittle Burns's prose because of such insipid sentimentalities as the worst letters to Clarinda, is to treat him with unfairness. He was not as consistently brilliant a letter-writer as, say, Byron; but when he was free from the restraints imposed by social inequality, and was unhampered by his own amatory propensities, he wrote letters that have not yet lost their tang and sparkle.

Burns once entrusted Peggy Chalmers with his formula for success in this intimate form of art. "Write whatever comes first," he told her; "what you see, what you read, what you hear, what you admire, what you dislike; trifles, bagatelles, nonsense; or, to fill up a corner, e'en put down a laugh at full length." But he himself followed no such hit-or-miss rule. Letter-writing he knew to be a serious and difficult matter. Preliminary drafts, carefully revised, prove how scrupulously he considered details of style; numerous copies made for friends show how eager he was to be known for his skill in prose.

It would be a pleasant task to quote at length from Burns's letters, and thus to demonstrate the merit he was sure they possessed. But I limit myself to one little-known but amusing paragraph addressed to the irascible William Nicol, who had lent Burns his bay mare, "Peg Nicholson". Burns was to use her in his Ellisland ploughing and then to sell her for the benefit of her owner, who had no need for a horse while teaching Latin in the Edinburgh High School. But the Ellisland venture proved even worse for Peg Nicholson than for Burns. Consequently, on February 9, 1790, Burns wrote thus to Nicol:

That d-mned mare of yours is dead. . . . I refused

fifty-five shillings for her, which was the highest bode I could squeeze for her. I fed her up and had her in fine order for Dumfries fair; when four or five days before the fair, she was seized with an unaccountable disorder in the sinews, or somewhere in the bones of the neck; with a weakness or total want of power in her fillets; and, in short, the whole vertebrae of her spine seemed to be diseased and unhinged; and in eight and forty hours, in spite of the two best farriers in the country, she died and be d-mned to her.

It is good fooling, such a paragraph, and illustrates Burns's fondness for a little nonsense, as well as his skill in writing an entertaining sort of prose. And if one will turn the pages of the letters to Ainslie, Cunningham, Margaret Chalmers, Cleghorn, or James Johnson, for example, one will see that this skill extended far beyond the field of humorous anecdote, and that Burns, speaking in his own idiom to sympathetic and understanding readers, had a genuine gift of style in prose.

The best of these letters also show the ease with which Burns wrote English, which some of his interpreters would have us believe was a foreign tongue to him. Like every educated Scotsman of his day, he read his English Bible, knew the great documents of English literature, and habitually used English in the serious business of life. He understood that since at least 1604 the English language had belonged to Edinburgh as well as to London. His early studies had been concerned with English models. When he himself began to write, he inevitably used English. As a result he developed a genuine command of English before he had really tried his hand at Scots; indeed, the only pieces of vernacular prose he ever wrote are obvious *tours de force*. Hence, when one says that Burns could write good prose, one means that he could write good English prose.

The situation is not quite so clear as regards Burns's poetry. He himself said, "These English songs gravel me to death". Taken by and large, his best poems, if not always predominantly Scottish, are at least flavoured with the vernacular. His least effective ones are pure English. Observing these facts, readers have hurried to the conclusion that Burns could not write good poetry in English.

On such a generalization two comments seem pertinent. First, Burns not only could but did write effective poetry in English. If you doubt me, open the book and see. Take, for example, the last song in *The Jolly Beggars*, beginning, "See the smoking bowl before us". It is English from beginning to end. Or choose something very different, *My Love is like a Red, Red Rose*—one of the perfectly cut and polished gems in Burns's song collection. Four touches of the vernacular—*bonie*, *gang*, *a'*, and *weel*—are all that save the song from being pure English. *Sweet Afton* shows no syllable of Scots; the vernacular in *Scots Wha Hae* is negligible, and disappears entirely as the poem rises to its climax in the last two stanzas. The marvellous quatrain beginning "Had we never lov'd sae kindly" contains no Scots except the *sae* substituted for *so*. Now these are not unusual examples, so far as their language is concerned; they are typical of much that Burns wrote in either unadulterated English or in an English barely tinged with a suggestion of Scottish dialect. And there is enough poetic merit in these and similar passages definitely to overthrow the old misconception that when Burns wrote English poetry he wrote poor poetry.

Second, if anyone asks why so much of Burns's poor work is in English, the answer is not far to seek. When he wrote English, he patterned his work after English poets who were high in esteem, but with whom, unfortunately, he had virtually nothing in common except language. In trying to imitate them he was attempting the impossible, but the resulting failure was not due to linguistic difficulties.

All this about Burns's vocabulary, gift of phrase, command of prose, and ability to write English, is not without significance in a study of Burns's art; but the world knows him as a poet, and it is by his poetry that his memory will be kept alive, if indeed it is to attain the immortality so hopefully predicted for it. Hence it will be well to give over these preliminaries, and to come to grips at once with our major problem, the bases of Burns's claim to distinction as an artist.

Consider first his metrical skill. In the *Epistle to James Smith*, Burns, like many another youthful poet, offered a prayer for supernatural assistance. Wisely enough he made his petition quite specific: "Give me", he said, "ay rowth—abundance—o' rhymes!" If the Powers who dispense favours to the sons of Apollo ever grant such petitions, they did so in the case of Burns. Forgetting for the moment both the intellectual content and the emotional values of Burns's poetry, and considering it solely as sounds put together in various rhythmic patterns, one finds in it the clearest evidence that by 1785 Burns had become an astonishingly brilliant technician. The mechanics of verse seem almost never to have bothered him.

I say "almost never". Burns did nothing significant in blank verse, the heroic couplet, or the sonnet. Why he avoided these popular forms it would be hard to say, but the fact is clear and needs no interpretation or further comment. Similarly, the Spenserian stanza, attempted with reasonable success in *The Cotter's Saturday Night*, was perhaps too languourous in its cadences to fit easily into the mood of Burns's swiftly moving intellect; he used it rarely thereafter. But in the eight-syllable couplet of *The Twa Dogs*, the nine-line stanza of *The Holy Fair*, and the six-line stanza of *To a Mouse*, in these three often-used staves Burns moved with consummate ease, and with a varied richness of effect that prevents any suggestion of monotony. And when his work carried him into the field of Scottish song, he found the most intricate patterns as easy to master as the simplest.

Such generalizations mean little unless enforced by specific illustrations, and to illustrate the range and technical excellence of Burns's metrics would require more extensive quotation than can be indulged in here. But three or four citations will certainly be in point. Consider a characteristic stanza of *The Holy Fair:*

> Here some are thinkin on their sins,
>   An' some upo' their claes;
> Ane curses feet that fyled his shins,
>   Anither sighs an' prays:
> On this hand sits a chosen swatch,
>   Wi' screwed-up, grace-proud faces;
> On that a set o' chaps at watch,
>   Thrang winkin on the lasses
>   To chairs that day.

The poem is composed of twenty-seven of these stanzas, each closing with a four-syllable "tag" or "tail" that ends in the word *day;* and in every one of the twenty-seven stanzas the full meaning is held in suspense till the final phrase, like "unkend that day", "wi' fright that day", or "a lift that day", has furnished the logical as well as the metrical conclusion. To carry a poem successfully through half a dozen such stanzas would test the ingenuity of most writers; to continue this feat through a poem as long as *The Holy Fair*, and to make each tag seem not like a refrain, or a phrase tacked on artificially, but like the only possible conclusion for the stanza, is to demonstrate a skill which one would call virtuosity were not the difficulty so adroitly concealed. And Burns accomplished this feat not only in *The Holy Fair* but in several other poems built on the same pattern.

Or look at *The Jolly Beggars*. The poem as we know it consists of sixteen parts. Eight are songs, and eight "recitativos", as Burns called them: descriptive sections which furnish the frame-work for the whole, introduce and characterize the various participants, and recount the incidental action in the poem. The first and last of the "recitativos" are in the same form—the intricate bob-wheel stanza which Montgomery's *Cherry and the Slae* had introduced to Scotland; but the other fourteen sections are cast in fourteen different moulds, varying all the way from a simple eight-syllable iambic quatrain to the thirteeners of the soldier's song, with their elaborate internal rhymes, and the binding-rhyme of *drum* running through the entire poem:

> I am a son of Mars who have been in many wars,
>   And show my cuts and scars wherever I come;
> This here was for a wench, and that other in a trench
>   When welcoming the French at the sound of a drum.

Burns was fond of a single rhyme uniting all the stanzas of a poem; he used the device often, and never gave any indication that the difficulty in which it involved him was any handicap to the success he almost always attained.

"I rhyme for fun", he said in the *Epistle to James Smith*. Apparently the fun increased with the difficulty of the task; for when, as in the first Bard's song of the *Beggars*, he found his ideas taking shape as a series of simple quatrains, he introduced internal rhymes by way of good measure:

> I am a Bard of no regard
>   Wi' gentle-folk and a' that;
> But Homer-like the glowrin' byke
>   Frae town to town I draw that.
>
> I never drank the Muses' stank,
>   Castalia's burn, an' a' that;
> But there it streams, an' richly reams—
>   My Helicon I ca' that.

There is such a lavishness about Burns's prosody, such a revelling in difficulties surmounted, such a playful delight in unexpected, elaborate, but appropriate rhymes, that one hardly knows where to turn to find their parallel. *On Glenriddell's Fox Breaking his Chain* is not one of the poems by which Burns will be remembered, but he must have chuckled with delight as he wrote it. There is good history in it, by the way, as well as evidence of metrical skill:

> Sir Reynard daily heard debates
> Of princes', kings', and nations' fates,
> With many rueful, bloody stories
> Of tyrants, Jacobites, and Tories:
> From liberty how angels fell,
> That now are galley-slaves in Hell;
> How Nimrod first the trade began
> Of binding Slavery's chains on man;
> How fell Semiramis—God damn her!—
> Did first, with sacrilegious hammer
> (All ills till then were trivial matters)
> For man dethron'd forge hen-peck fetters;
> How Xerxes, that abandoned Tory,
> Thought cutting throats was reaping glory,
> Until the stubborn Whigs of Sparta
> Taught him great Nature's Magna Charta.

The *Lament for the Absence of William Creech* closes with an astonishing stanza that Lowell might have been reading when he characterized himself in *A Fable for Critics:*

> May never wicked Fortune touzle him,
> May never wicked men bamboozle him,

> Until a pow as auld's Methusalem
> He canty claw!
> Then to the blessed new Jerusalem
> Fleet-wing awa!

Fun indeed such writing must have been!

Obviously it was easy for Burns to cast his ideas into metrical patterns. In doing so, moreover, he rarely failed to select a verse-form appropriate to his material, and thus to achieve that happy union of form and content which is one of the goals of all art. In the songs, indeed, three factors instead of two combine to make the total effect; and only when idea, metrical pattern, and melody have all contributed their parts to the whole, only then does the full value of Burns's work become apparent.

It would be a vain quest to search Burns's poetry for many examples of such perfect tone and texture as distinguish the best work of, say, Tennyson or Wordsworth. He wrote hurriedly, had little time for revision, and as a rule paid scant attention to the finer shadings of vocalic and consonantal values. But even these were not always overlooked. A song of two stanzas, *The Silver Tassie*, bears witness to Burns's interest in such refinements of technique:

> Go fetch to me a pint o' wine
> And fill it in a silver tassie

> That I may drink before I go
>   A service to my bonie lassie!
> The boat rocks at the pier o' Leith,
>   Fu' loud the wind blaws frae the Ferry,
> The ship rides by the Berwick-Law,
>   And I maun leave my bonie Mary.
>
> The trumpets sound, the banners fly,
>   The glittering spears are ranked ready,
> The shouts o' war are heard afar,
>   The battle closes deep and bloody.
> It's not the roar o' sea or shore
>   Wad make me langer wish to tarry,
> Nor shouts o' war that's heard afar:
>   It's leaving thee, my bonie Mary.

Whoever is tempted to believe that Burns's art was largely intuitive, should pay careful attention to the second stanza of that song, with its effective crescendo, and its careful modulation of such sounds as best fit the mood and suggest the idea.

One need look no further, I take it, for indications of Burns's metrical skill. The evidence is conclusive. Whether his mood was light-hearted, or wistful, or bitter, whether he was dealing with the trivialities of an hour or the enduring values of human life, seemed to make no difference. So far as the mechanics of verse were concerned, he was an assured master of his craft.

But craftsmanship, important as it is in any art, can hardly be counted on to preserve Burns's memory to eternity. One admires the technique of those oriental workers in ivory who carve spheres within spheres; and yet one realizes that theirs is a lifeless art, devoid of genuine human significance. Fortunately for Burns's reputation, his fame rests on more substantial bases than command of metrical form. Each of the three fields in which he did his most characteristic work—the songs, the satires, the narrative and descriptive poems—yields a rich harvest to one who seeks evidence concerning Burns's art.

In thinking of Burns's songs, one remembers that most of them were written relatively late in his life. As a lad he had begun his literary career with a song, to be sure, and from time to time during what might be called his apprenticeship he had composed many more. But not until after the Kilmarnock and Edinburgh volumes had brought him fame, and James Johnson had interested him in the *Scots Musical Museum*, did he set himself seriously to the happy task that was to engage him for the rest of his life. Once committed to the task, however, he kept enthusiastically at it till he had produced the astonishing total of three hundred and fifty-four songs—a body of lyrics such as seems never to have come from the pen of any other significant English or American poet.[1] For many of these Burns drew heavily

[1] This is the number admitted by J. C. Dick to his *Songs of Robert Burns with the Melodies for which they were Written* (London, 1903). There are, of course, a number of high-kilted songs which Dick felt constrained not to print.

upon already existing material; but always he added more than he borrowed. The finished product was Burns's, and no one's else.

Inevitably, there are many songs in a collection as large as this that seem ineffective, and many more that are but mediocre. The years in which Burns was writing his songs were heavy with the burden of family and business cares, and clouded by the shadow of grave illness. Consequently he did not a little work that is of no lasting significance —though one should add that some of the songs which appear commonplace when merely read from the printed page, disclose a considerable merit when properly sung to the tunes for which they were written. But the student of Burns's art will begin his examination of the songs by eliminating two-thirds of them from serious consideration.

When one has made this exclusion, however, one finds remaining two groups of songs that will repay all the attention one can give them: a number of somewhat conventional lyrics, each of which is made memorable by a stanza or quatrain of obvious distinction; and a small sheaf of songs, dealing with different moods or themes or phases of human experience, in which Burns has come close to that perfection which every artist hopes to attain. In the first group I place songs like *Ae Fond Kiss* and *Mary Morison*, which break down under close scrutiny. The former is marked by a turgidity that contrasts sharply with the simplicity of Burns's best work. But the last quatrain of the second stanza would save any song from oblivion. Similarly, *Mary Morison* carries a heavy freight of conventional phraseology: "the trysted hour", "the miser's treasure", "the weary slave", "wreck his peace". The second stanza, however, is one of those flawless things of which any poet would be proud:

> Yestreen, when to the trembling string
>   The dance gaed thro' the lighted ha',
> To thee my fancy took its wing,
>   I sat, but neither heard nor saw;
> Tho' this was fair, and that was braw,
>   And yon the toast of a' the town,
> I sigh'd, and said amang them a':—
>   "Ye are na Mary Morison."

But, of course, the songs by which Burns will be longest remembered show no such unevenness as appears in *Ae Fond Kiss* and *Mary Morison*. They are the songs in which Burns reached at once a high level of lyric accomplishment and maintained that level to the close. There are not many in the group, but there are enough so that, were all the others wiped out of existence, we should still think of Burns as one of our foremost song-writers. They are built around many themes: friendship, democracy, patriotism, love of liberty, delight in "a night of good fellowship", and love;

love of man for woman, of woman for man, the comedy of love, the tragedy of love, and the enduring beauty and significance of love. No two people would agree as to just what songs belong in this group; but *Whistle and I'll Come to You, My Lad*, and *The Silver Tassie*, and *John Anderson My Jo*, and *Willie Brew'd a Peck o' Maut*, and *Tam Glen*, and *A Red, Red Rose*, and *Auld Lang Syne*, and *Scots Wha Hae*, and *Bonie Doon*, and *A Man's a Man for A' That*—these at least would receive many votes. "Simple, sensuous, and impassioned", covering a wide range of human experience, good when read and better when sung, these songs show Burns's lyric powers at their height.

    John Anderson my jo, John,
      When we were first acquent,
    Your locks were like the raven,
      Your bonie brow was brent;
    But now your brow is beld, John,
      Your locks are like the snaw;
    But blessings on your frosty pow,
      John Anderson my jo.

    John Anderson my jo, John,
      We clamb the hill thegither,
    And monie a cantie day, John,
      We've had wi' ane anither;
    Now we maun totter down, John,
      But hand in hand we'll go,
    And sleep thegither at the foot,
      John Anderson my jo.

If this be not art, I do not know what art may be.

Turn for a moment to Burns's satires. It is a commonplace that, though the satiric mood seems one of the enduring concomitants of human life, any particular literary expression of this mood may soon cease to be intelligible, and so may lose much of its value as a work of art. An effective satire, aimed directly at certain conditions of the hour, has a local or temporary value which is often forgotten when the conditions that occasioned the satire have ceased to exist. When allusions or figures of speech need extensive explanation in footnotes, the time is not far distant when only the literary historian will consider the work important. But if the satire deals with some fundamental trait of human nature, and takes such form that changing conditions do not destroy or conceal its effectiveness, then, like the best pages of Aristophanes and Swift, it may attain a long-continuing significance.

Many of Burns's satires have unquestionably lost their effectiveness through the mere passing of time. His strongly partisan political verses, intended to influence particular election contests, are virtually unintelligible to the general reader, and demand copious annotation for even the specialist. Such vigorous pieces as *The Twa Herds*, *The Kirk's Alarm*, and *The Address of Beelzebub*, though clear enough in their general import, are yet so specific in their treatment of purely local situations that they, too, can hardly be read without an elaborate commentary. Even *The Holy Fair*, that superb combination of "playful banter, mordant irony, broad comedy, and subtle sarcasm", loses much of its point unless one knows a good deal about the local celebrities whom the poem caricatures. But once, in *Holy Willie's Prayer*, Burns wrote satire which seems immune to the wasting influence of time. No one cares who the specific victim was; Gavin Hamilton and Robert Aiken, to whom Holy Willie refers, need no identification. Burns's interest in such local personalities was only incidental. The major objectives of his attack, in military idiom, were first, the basic dogmas of Calvinism—original sin, universal damnation, and election; and second, that peculiarly offensive sort of hypocrisy which sometimes goes arm in arm with religious zeal. William Fisher merely happened to be the aiming-point for Burns's barrage. Like the fortunate souls whom Calvin believed elected for salvation, this poem seems marked for immortality; men will read it as long as they retain an interest in dogmatic theology or find hypocrisy offensive, and they will discover in it every quality that great satire should possess: the significant idea expressed in appropriate and mirth-provoking form; the brilliant and daring phrase; the flawless rhythm;

the picturesque and sensuous imagery; and, fusing all into a perfect whole, that blend of laughter and *saeva indignatio* which the author's restraint and self-control make doubly effective. Again I say, if *Holy Willie's Prayer* be not art, then there is no art in satire.

Among the large number of Burns's poems which may be roughly characterized as narrative or descriptive, there is no one which occupies the position of obvious pre-eminence that *Holy Willie's Prayer* has won for itself among the satires; but the critic who selects *Tam* and *The Jolly Beggars* to illustrate Burns's accomplishment in this large domain of poetry, will find few people objecting to his choice.

To call *Tam* a superlatively good ghost story is to concede that it is not the greatest sort of poetry, and also to admit it to some kind of spiritual kinship with *The Ancient Mariner*, which seems easily first among all versified ghost stories. The two poems have much in common: a quiet, almost matter-of-fact opening, a steady heightening of the emotional pitch, a superb climax, and a swift conclusion, rounded off by a brief, moralizing tag. Each rises deftly, like a well-piloted aeroplane, from the solid earth of human experience to the thin atmosphere of supernatural adventure; each shows a firmly spun thread of narrative linking together brilliant descriptive passages: from Coleridge's pen those magical vignettes of sea and sky and setting sun; from Burns's, the sketch of alehouse and ruined kirk, and such a thunder-storm as not even Coleridge ever equalled. Our old-fashioned text-books on rhetoric might well have used either poem to illustrate the fine arts of narration and description.

But the mood of *Tam* is utterly different from that of *The Ancient Mariner*. Coleridge, with Wordsworth at his elbow, wrote his masterpiece in characteristically serious vein, gave it the place of honour at the forefront of the *Lyrical Ballads*, and revised it extensively for a subsequent printing. Burns, lighthearted and mirthful, tossed off *Tam* to gratify Francis Grose's interest in Scottish "antiquities". "Print my piece or not, as you think proper", he told Grose when sending him the manuscript. When Grose published it merely as a footnote to his own prose—and prosaic—description of Alloway Kirk, Burns made no protest. One wonders whether a more notable footnote has ever dignified the bottom of any page.

The history of *The Jolly Beggars* illustrates even better than *Tam* the casual way in which Burns treated his work. Written in 1785 or 1786, and omitted from the 1787 volume on the advice of Hugh Blair, the poem passed from Burns's mind till Thomson questioned him about it in 1793. Then he said, "I have forgotten the cantata you allude to, as I kept no copy, and, indeed, did not know that it was in existence; however, I remember that none of the songs pleased myself except the last—something about

> Courts for cowards were erected,
> Churches built to please the priest."

Others than Burns himself have paid relatively slight attention to *The Jolly Beggars*. I remember my surprise and perplexity when two years ago a distinguished Scottish man of letters and scholar said to me: "We Scots don't care much for *The Jolly Beggars*; it is the English and Americans who praise it." Strange as the remark seemed to me at the time, I am inclined on reflection to believe that it stated the case accurately; for *The Jolly Beggars* is not one of the poems that Scottish critics have applauded most vigorously. Specifically Scottish elements in the poem are few. Granted that it was occasioned by a glimpse of a ragged company sheltering under Agnes Gibson's roof in Mauchline village; granted that its language is strongly flavoured with the vernacular; the fact still remains that the

> merry core
> O' randie gangrel bodies

whom Burns described are no more Scottish than Banquo and Macbeth. They are kin to Bret Harte's "Outcasts of Poker Flat" and to Kipling's

"Broken Men". They are the pariahs of all lands and all ages. The poem is one of the glories of Scottish literature, but the subject-matter is as universal as poverty and misfortune, and the instinct to find solace for such woes in human companionship.

Scottish readers, seeking and finding in Burns poetic idealization of distinctively Scottish themes, have failed, perhaps, to recognize the true worth of *The Jolly Beggars*. Here Matthew Arnold's judgment was right. His somewhat atrophied sense of humour estopped him from appreciating Burns's delight in comic incongruities; his Oxonian dislike of "Scotch religion, Scotch manners, and Scotch drink" was a bar to the enjoyment of much that readers less close to the summit of Olympus have found thoroughly delightful. But his instinctive appreciation of a work of creative imagination conquered even his Johnsonian aversion to things Caledonian, and concerning *The Jolly Beggars* he was fairer to Burns than some of the poet's countrymen have been. It is in truth what Arnold called it, "a puissant and splendid production".

Here, as in *Tam*, one finds a flawless metrical technique; here, too, is a dramatic narrative, interspersed with descriptive passages which show Burns's pictorial skill at its height; here are characterizations of men and women as vivid and memorable almost as Chaucer's portraits; and here, blending the sixteen sections into a unit, is a throbbing joy in what life has to offer, as well as a passionate protest against some of the inequalities of life's offerings. The poem towers over Gay's *Beggars' Opera*, with which it is sometimes compared, as Edinburgh Castle would tower over the Royal Crescent at Bath.

Thinking over the entire range of Burns's art, one observes certain qualities or characteristics that appear like common denominators in each of the three fields that we have glanced at. Quite obviously, it was a rapidly developing art. Without being able accurately to date all of Burns's early poetry, one can say with assurance that before 1784 he had done little work of distinction; by the close of 1786 he had to his credit all of the Kilmarnock edition, and unpublished poems which would have made at least as notable a volume as that which John Wilson printed.

It was, too, an uneven and inconsistent art. "Of all boring matters in this boring world", Burns once wrote to George Thomson, "criticizing my own work is the greatest bore." As a result of this distaste for scrutinizing what he had written, and of the press of circumstances that during all his life deprived him of the leisure for careful composition, Burns published good and bad in close juxtaposition. Four lines in *The Cotter's Saturday Night* illustrate the way Burns not infrequently put black and white together within a single poem:

> The parents, partial, eye their hopeful years;
> Anticipation forward points the view;
> The mother, wi' her needle an' her sheers,
> Gars auld claes look amaist as weel's the new.

If the first two lines be not Burns at his absolute worst, they seem so by contrast with the simplicity and veracity of the last two. The unevenness apparent in this excerpt is typical of an unevenness that marks Burns's work as a whole.

Again, Burns's verse is pronouncedly imitative—a fact which accounts for much of its unevenness. Like every youthful poet, he looked about for models, and selected some that were appropriate and some that were quite the reverse. When he took his cues from Ramsay and Fergusson and the unknown authors of Scottish song, he was soon surpassing their best work; when he imitated Collins's *Ode to the Memory of James Thomson*, he failed. But, in failure and success alike, Burns owed much to the examples of earlier writers.

One should add, however, that never was Burns a mere copyist, setting up his easel before a masterpiece and endeavouring to reproduce it; always he added something of his own—a deftly turned phrase, a stanza for which he alone was responsible, or that mysterious something which every reader is conscious of, but which no reader can adequately characterize—that touch of style which only genius can impart to a printed page. Francis Sempill's and Allan Ramsay's versions of *Auld Lang Syne* were well enough in their way, but they would have been forgotten long ago if Burns had not shown by how much the pupil can excel the master:

> We twa hae run about the braes,
>   And pu'd the gowans fine,
> But we've wander'd monie a weary fit
>   Sin' auld lang syne.
>
> We twa hae paidl'd in the burn
>   Frae morning sun till dine,
> But seas between us braid hae roar'd
>   Sin' auld lang syne.

Except in Burns's other work, nothing in all Scottish song has quite the touch of magic that Burns imparted to those two stanzas. Fergusson's *Leith Races* is a vivid and entertaining picture of one phase of "Scotch manners"; but *The Holy Fair*, which Burns modelled on Fergusson's poem, is superior to it in every respect. For *The Jolly Beggars*, Burns drew generously upon published songs and sketches dealing with jovial mumpers and gaberlunzies. But all are forgotten, except as they appear in such places as Henley and Henderson's notes to Burns's cantata. Wherever one turns, one finds the same result: the originality in Burns overshadows all the evidence of imitation.

And, finally, in this best of Burns, one discovers, unquestionably as it seems to me, a great art. No *Hamlet* ever came from Burns's pen, no *Paradise Lost*, no *Divine Comedy*. But had Burns never written anything except *To a Mouse*, we could still have said that he possessed a great and original genius, which found expression in noble poetry. Here, if anywhere in literature, is exemplified the glory of the commonplace, the significance of the ordinary. Here, if anywhere in literature, one sees a most trivial incident so recounted and so interpreted as to become a symbol of abiding truth. The episode must have taken place unnumbered times, but during all the centuries in which men have tilled their fields, no poet except Burns had had enough penetrative imagination to see the tragedy of the mouse in its true significance. One ploughman, driving his share through the cunningly built nest, stamps with a heavy boot and moves on to the end of the furrow. Another, looking down on the mouse tangled in the debris of leaves and stubble, seizes a clod and hurls it. Only to Burns was it given to discover in the mouse his own "earth-born companion and fellow mortal", and to see in her fate a symbol of his own. Deny it one hardly can: mouse and poet and reader alike are earth-born, and born to die; how much they have in common! One may praise the poem on the score of this imaginative veracity, or as an illustration of

Burns's accurate observation, or as further proof of his technical skill. One may point out the felicity of phrase, or note the restraint which Burns exercised over his fondness for sentimentalizing and indulging in heroics. But all these considerations and many more are powerless to explain the moving effectiveness of the poem, particularly of the closing stanzas, where Burns deftly shifts the reader's attention from the mouse to the poet, and thus to some of the unsolved problems of universal human experience. By this time the light-heartedness of the opening stanzas has all disappeared; the shadows of a November twilight deepen over the field where reader and poet stand together and muse:

> But, Mousie, thou art no thy lane
> In proving foresight may be vain;
> The best-laid schemes o' mice an' men
>   Gang aft a-gley,
> An' lea'e us nought but grief an' pain
>   For promis'd joy.
>
> Still thou art blest, compar'd wi' me!
> The present only toucheth thee:
> But, och! I backward cast my e'e
>   On prospects drear!
> An' forward, tho' I canna see,
>   I guess, an' fear!

Would it be a rash prophecy to say that these lines will be remembered as long as heart-broken men and women review the past with regret, or await the future with misgiving?

To return, then, to the question with which we began: "How well can Burns write; is he merely a facile rhymester; or is he really an artist?" Can there be any uncertainty about the answer? Whether one looks at songs, satires, or narrative and descriptive poems, the result is the same: one finds much that only a great artist could possibly have produced. And I am glad to put myself on record as believing that, for this reason, the chairmen of future anniversary dinners need have little hesitancy about proposing the toast to "the immortal memory of Robert Burns!"

OHIO UNIVERSITY LIBRARY

Please return this